N A W I L I W I L I
K I P U
R. P. 4477 Kamamalu V.
R. P. 4478 Kamamalu V.
1094 Acres
Alakoko Pond
Kauai Industrial School
Mill

GROVE FARM, KAUA'I

150 Years of Stewardship and Innovation

Aloha
Michael & Linda

GROVE FARM, KAUA'I

150 Years of Stewardship and Innovation

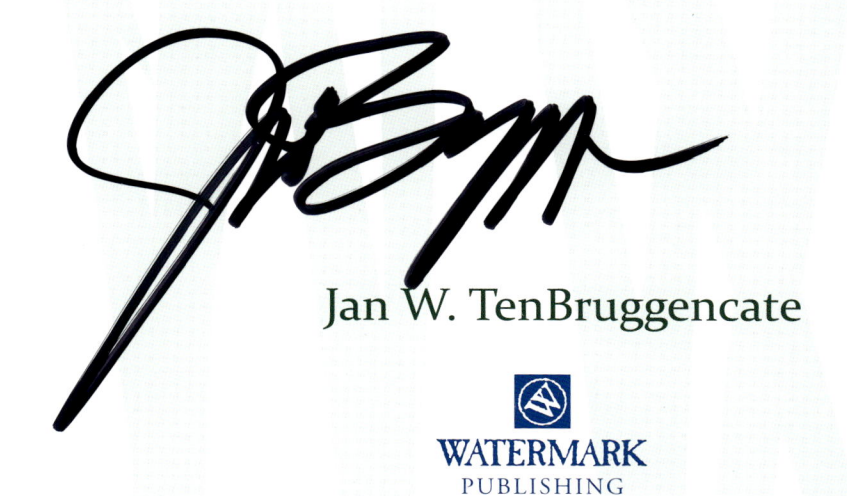

Jan W. TenBruggencate

WATERMARK PUBLISHING

© 2014 Grove Farm

All rights reserved. No part of this book may be reproduced in any form or by any electronic or mechanical means, including information retrieval systems, without prior written permission from the publisher, except for brief passages quoted in reviews.

ISBN 978-1-935690-61-0

Library of Congress Control Number: 2014954310

Design and production by Kurt Osaki and Stacy Fujitani, Osaki Creative Group

Archival photography from Grove Farm Homestead Museum; aerial photography by Nick Galante; supplemental photography by Marissa Sandblom, Rhye Daub, Royce Kawabata and Carol Ann Davis (pp. 72-73)

For bulk orders, contact:
Grove Farm
3-1850 Kaumualii Hwy.
Lihue, HI 96766-8609

For single-copy orders, contact:
Watermark Publishing
1000 Bishop St., Ste. 806
Honolulu, HI 96813
Toll-free 1-866-900-BOOK
sales@bookshawaii.net
www.bookshawaii.net

Printed in Korea

Contents

1	**Foreword**
2	**Introduction**
4	**Chapter One** Grove Farm, The Innovator
34	**Chapter Two** Koloa Plantation
52	**Chapter Three** Lihue Plantation
64	**Chapter Four** Growing Up Grove Farm
72	**Chapter Five** The Troubles
86	**Chapter Six** Selling Grove Farm
98	**Chapter Seven** The Initiatives
122	**Epilogue**
124	**Grove Farm Archive**
142	**Bibliography**
144	**Index**

Foreword

The Grove Farm of 150 years ago is very different from today's Grove Farm, and yet in many ways it is very familiar.

Grove Farm today is an amalgam of former sugar plantations. The oldest portion is the former Koloa Sugar Company, which also grew sugar cane for Grove Farm and McBryde Sugar Company. Second oldest is the Lihue Plantation portion, which dates to just a few years before Grove Farm's founding. And then there's the core plantation, Grove Farm, a relative youngster compared to Koloa's 179-year history and Lihue's 165 years.

Grove Farm's founder, George Norton Wilcox, was a man who realized he needed to build the community at the same time he built the company. He saw that building infrastructure and the island's economy was part of that. He recognized that he had to support education, that he had to reforest the land, that he should serve in government when called, that he should support his employees and also help the needy.

In many ways, the Case family's goals for the plantation and the community are mirror images of those of G.N. Wilcox:

"My dad's legacy and to some extent our family legacy lives on. We're trying to be good stewards and good citizens of the community, trying to do some things that move things forward," Steve Case said.

Today, Grove Farm's innovative initiatives in community building, ecological restoration, preservation of habitats, diversified agriculture and renewable energy continue to lead Kaua'i in much the same way that Wilcox did. In addition, a well-funded Grove Farm Foundation serves the community. Grove Farm employees participate in community activities, and the company leads many community-wide efforts for the benefit of Kaua'i. Given today's media, these efforts are communicated and known in real time.

In G.N. Wilcox's day, it was all very private. He once took a steamer to O'ahu to quietly deposit funds into a retired employee's account. He would make massive gifts to educational and other institutions—often insisting on anonymity. He was a soft touch—his employees knew that the best time to ask for a raise was right after Wilcox had yelled at you for something—because he would feel guilty about it.

When Steve Case bought Grove Farm in 2000, he bought Hawaiian sugar history. His goal, my goal and that of everyone in the company is to continue the legacy of innovation, collaboration, sustainability and giving to make our beloved Kaua'i a better place.

—Warren H. Haruki, President, Grove Farm

FOREWORD 1

Introduction

"Things done at Grove Farm were innovative—water irrigation, blasting through the mountain—leveraging technology as they tried to determine a better way to meet their objectives." —Steve Case

There are themes that run through Grove Farm; themes passed down through changes in ownership, changes in management, changes in technology, changes in sources of revenue, changes in community and even through the changes in Hawaiian government from monarchy to republic, to territory to state. Why do these themes persist? Perhaps, in part, it is because Grove Farm is a family affair. Always has been.

The structure has been altered, certainly. It went from a big plantation owned entirely by a single individual—George Norton Wilcox—to a Wilcox family-held corporation, to a more widely-held corporation that included non-family members and today, is back to ownership by one man—this time Steve Case.

Childless George Norton Wilcox brought his siblings and his nephews and nieces into the company early. Their children and grandchildren continued to run it after his death. The Wilcoxes were in control of the company for 136 years, from 1864 to Case's purchase in 2000. But they were far from the only family whose history is woven through the company's story.

There was a period just a generation ago when the company's president was founder George N. Wilcox's grandnephew, Sam Wilcox. Its plantation manager was David Pratt, grandson of former Grove Farm manager E.H.W. Broadbent and son of former Grove Farm attorney Dudley Pratt Sr. And corporate counsel was Dan Case, son of former company treasurer "Hib" Case.

In the working ranks, Pat Agustin was a journeyman painter for Grove Farm, where his dad had been a contract irrigator. Michiye Funaku ran data systems at Grove Farm, where her father had been a railroad tracklayer. Perfecto Labrador was a diesel mechanic at Grove Farm, and his dad had been a stable master for Koloa Sugar, which was acquired by Grove Farm. And those are just a few of the multi-generation Grove Farm families.

Owner Steve Case bought Grove Farm with the fortune he amassed at AOL Time Warner, but his own roots at Grove Farm go back most of a century.

Steve Case's grandfather, Hib, came to Grove Farm shortly after World War I as an agriculturist and remained with the company his entire career as a bookkeeper and later corporate treasurer, living for many of those years in the home that came to be known as the Grove Farm Manager's House, whose driveways were lined in royal palms.

Steve's father, Dan, was born on Kaua'i and spent his boyhood playing in Grove Farm's fields and valleys. Dan later became Grove Farm's corporate attorney. And Steve Case himself is an island boy—raised on O'ahu but spending many summers on Kaua'i.

At this writing, Dan Case sits on the Grove Farm Board of Directors. So does former company president David Pratt. Pratt spent his summers playing around his grandfather's Līhu'e home, as well as at the family cabin in the mountains at Kōke'e. Pratt's sons are Wilcoxes by virtue of his first wife Debbie, the daughter of Pratt's predecessor as Grove Farm president, Sam Wilcox.

Is it any wonder that Grove Farm remains true to its roots?

It's a family thing.

George Norton Wilcox recognized this by bringing his family into the company he built. Steve Case recognizes it by carrying forward many of the same ideas that drove the man who was known to business associates as Mr. Wilcox, but as Keoki or even Makule Georgie, or Old George, to his neighbors of many ethnicities.

"The connection to the past is important, not just from the legacy-heritage-respect format, but because the legacy of the past helps inform the future," Steve Case said.

In preparing this volume, the author owes debts of gratitude to numerous friends of Grove Farm who gave time and were patient with questions. This book would not have been possible without the many people who hold in their minds and their hearts the history of Grove Farm, and the Koloa and Lihue Plantations.

Chief among them is my collaborator, Grove Farm vice president Marissa Sandblom, whose organizational skills are manifest, and to company secretary Sharyl Lam Yuen, who fulfilled every request for information on short notice. The company's board and management was very supportive, and I particularly thank Steve and Dan Case, David Pratt and his successor, Warren Haruki. Former Grove Farm chief operating officer Allan Smith provided valued perspective, as did former board member Donn Carswell.

The author also particularly thanks Shawn Shimabukuro, David Hinazumi, Arryl Kaneshiro and Gaylene and Boyd Gayagas. Bob Schleck, Moises Madayag, Remy Chinen and the staff at Grove Farm Homestead Museum were forgiving of my regular unannounced appearance and provided great assistance.

Moises did exemplary work scanning historic images. The extraordinary photographer Nick Galante hung out of a helicopter to capture some of the aerial shots in this book. Photographer Rhye Daub shot many of the color images at ground level.

And special thanks, of course, go to Pat Agustin, Bobby Agena, Chick Cacabelos, Michiye Funaku, David Nobriga, Perfecto Labrador, Bernie Sakoda, Carlina Vea, Remy Chinen and Stanley Viluan, who shared stories of the early days as plantation kids and as employees of Grove Farm.

There are innumerable unnamed others on Grove Farm's staff and throughout the community who provided perspective, and no book of this kind could have been completed without them. The team that produced this volume did its best to ensure accuracy of fact and perspective. Any errors are mine.

—Jan W. TenBruggencate

The old Grove Farm office is a metal-roofed, two-room structure nestled in the trees at today's Grove Farm Homestead Museum. George N. Wilcox often worked inside while his pack of dogs dozed on the lanai. The cottage where Wilcox slept is to the left. He left the main house to his brother, Sam, and Sam's children.

Chapter 1
Grove Farm, The Innovator

"(Capt.) Foster offered me an eighth share in the (schooner) C.R. Bishop and I took it, not because I thought it would ever pay, but because it was a good thing for the community to have a good vessel. That is the way I have made a good many of my investments, first and last."
—George N. Wilcox

"We are still trying to find the businesses that can work, can provide vitality to the community while continuing stewardship responsibly. How to use the land responsibly, how to create more jobs and homes. These things in any community are interconnected and particularly connected on an island." —Steve Case

Grove Farm is a company founded on innovation, and it actively continues its 150 years of innovation today. That all started with a locally born engineer named George Norton Wilcox, who had a knack for designing irrigation systems.

In the early 1800s, the lands inland from Nāwiliwili Bay were forested in native endemic trees and Polynesian-introduced forest species like the native lowland hardwood *koa*, the introduced *hau* in the wetlands, the native hardwood *'ahakea*, and— importantly for this story—the Polynesian-introduced candlenut *kukui*. Grove Farm started in a grove of kukui trees, and continues to claim kukui as a signature plant a century and a half later.

In all that time, the company's progress has been guided by just three entities—an individual owner, a family corporation and then another individual owner. Each of whose interests overlapped its neighbor, ensuring a continuity of purpose. Wilcox bought a small, struggling sugar farm from German immigrant Hermann Widemann, who would go on to serve on the Supreme Court of the Kingdom of Hawai'i. Wilcox, a child of missionaries, had no children of his own, and on his death he turned control of the company over to a corporation dominated by the descendants of his siblings. And when Grove Farm ran into financial trouble, it passed on to Steve Case, whose own family connection to Grove Farm dated back eighty years. Case was the grandson of the company's longtime bookkeeper A. Hebard Case. Steve Case's father, Dan, had grown up at Grove Farm, and helped oversee a continued vision. Steve himself had spent some of his summer vacations at Grove Farm.

Justice Widemann cut the initial sugar acreage out of a stand of kukui trees on land he bought for $8,000 in 1856 from James F.B. Marshall. Sugar had just begun striding into the leadership of the island kingdom's economy. The two great economic drivers of the late 1700s and early 1800s were whaling and sandalwood. But by the middle of the century both extractive mainstays faded, largely due to scarcity. Sandalwood crashed in the 1830s as *santalum* stands in Hawaiian forests thinned due to logging pressure. Whalers had similarly thinned the vast cetacean pods of the Pacific—and the discovery of petroleum on the American Mainland would complete the destruction of that industry. A number of Hawaiian industries—cattle among them—had been built on provisioning whaling fleets.

But sugar showed promise. Farmers were actively experimenting with the techniques that would turn it into an economic powerhouse. For Hanover-born Widemann, just thirty-two at the time, 1854 was a big year. He married native Hawaiian Kaumana Kapoli, known as Mary. The Hawaiian Kingdom— led by Hawai'i's longest-reigning monarch Kauikeaouli, Kamehameha III—named Widemann sheriff of the island. And he launched the concept of becoming a sugar planter on the plateau between Nāwiliwili and Puali Streams.

Planting cane was all the rage. On the other side of the Hoary Head Range, known in Hawaiian as Hā'upu, Koloa Plantation had gone through its growing pains and seemed on firm financial footing under the ownership of Robert Wood and Samuel Burbank. Just across Nāwiliwili Valley, William Harrison Rice was named manager of the five-year-old Lihue Plantation (it wasn't using that name

Top: Judge Hermann A. Widemann, who sold Grove Farm to G.N. Wilcox, with his daughter Minna in 1865. Widemann moved to Honolulu and became an influential figure in the Hawaiian government. Minna married another prominent Hawai'i resident, Jack Dowsett.
Bottom: In 1864 Judge Widemann put his sugar acreage and pastureland near Lihue Plantation up for sale. G.N. Wilcox leased the land from Widemann and later bought it outright.

yet), which had just finished construction of a new water-powered sugar mill.

And in 1857, a young George Norton Wilcox would begin work as a bookkeeper in Rice's plantation store. By 1863, Wilcox moved over to manage Grove Farm for Widemann. Widemann put the company up for sale in late 1864. Wilcox quickly determined to take it over, and in late 1865, he arranged to lease and later to buy the plantation from Widemann, who was moving to Honolulu to help run the Kingdom. Grove Farm considers 1864 to be the year the company started as a serious plantation.

The stories of Lihue Plantation, Koloa Plantation and Grove Farm would be interconnected for the entire 150 years of Grove Farm's history, leading ultimately to Grove Farm's acquisition of Koloa Plantation, and Steve Case's purchase of first Grove Farm and then the majority of Lihue Plantation's sugar lands.

On Nov. 5, 1864, Widemann placed an ad for the sale of his sugar farm in *The Pacific Commercial Advertiser*. It read:

To Let—"Grove Farm." At Nawiliwili, island of Kauai, containing 300 to 400 acres of best cane land, and about 500 acres of pasture land. The cane land and part of the pasture land can be watered. It is situated within a mile of Lihue Plantation Mill and 1¼ mile from the Landing Place. Roads excellent. There are three large enclosures for horses and cattle, and buildings sufficient for a large family, all in first-rate order and repair. Possession given immediately, if required. Terms low. For particulars, apply to H.A. WIDEMANN, or to HACKFELD & CO.

Clearly, the name Grove Farm existed before Wilcox was involved, and it may even have pre-dated Widemann and been used by the man from whom Widemann bought it in 1856, James Marshall. Marshall bought it in 1850 from Warren Goodale who had acquired the land immediately after private land ownership was authorized in the Islands through the Great Māhele.

But it is not clear it was an active sugar company before Wilcox. Grove Farm historians have debated that issue. Widemann had no apparent sugar cane milling capacity, and he is careful in his advertisement to refer to the sale of "cane land" rather than crop in the ground. He might have been growing some sugar cane, but he was certainly growing other crops as well. Grove Farm Homestead Museum still has, for example, the mill he used to make oil out of the kukui nuts that once covered the region.

Historian Bob Schleck, director of the museum, makes the distinction between the farm, which had ducks, chickens, pigs, housing and offices; and the plantation, which would grow the commercial crops like sugar, lychee, macadamia nuts, ti and pineapple. There are suggestions in the Grove Farm archives that Wilcox may have raised sheep for a brief period, but they never became a major part of the company's business.

What Widemann and Wilcox as sugar planters recognized long before most other sugar operations in the Islands was how critical irrigation was to their crop. Widemann mentions the potential to water the cane in his lease notice. He had engaged Wilcox to oversee the construction of a ditch system that would bring water to his sugar fields. Wilcox had studied civil engineering at the Sheffield Scientific School at Yale, in New Haven, Connecticut. And the evidence was that he was among the best irrigation engineers in the industry.

Wilcox moved quickly to sign a milling

In 1857, a young G.N. Wilcox began work as a bookkeeper in a plantation store.

Top: G.N. Wilcox's nieces and nephew, Mabel, Gaylord and Elsie, were raised at Grove Farm Homestead, the children of Wilcox's brother, Sam. Gaylord ran Grove Farm after G.N.'s death. Mabel built Grove Farm Homestead Museum on the old plantation headquarters farm.
Bottom: Wilcox's pack of dogs followed his horse when he rode the plantation as a young man and entertained him in his later years, as they do here in 1931.

GROVE FARM, THE INNOVATOR 7

agreement with his old employer at Lihue Plantation, and brought in workers to begin his own ditch system. It was a comparatively new concept for the Islands. Wilcox hired Hawaiian and Chinese workers to build a ditch and tunnel system from a dammed stream down to where the sugar grew. It was a breakthrough that immediately was imitated by sugar farmers around him, and Wilcox was personally called on to assist in the engineering of irrigation systems throughout the kingdom, including the massive East Maui irrigation system, which diverted dozens of streams and had the largest capacity of any irrigation system in the Islands.

The first irrigation ditch in the Hawaiian Islands is said to have been Lihue Plantation's Rice Ditch in 1856, which was marginally successful—it was so leaky that it conveyed no water in dry periods. It was later improved and formed the core of the plantation's irrigation systems. Wilcox followed in 1865 with Grove Farm's first ditch, which would itself be later straightened and lined to form Grove Farm's main ditch.

The ditch brought water from Kilohana Crater, a 900-foot-elevation volcanic crater inland from Līhu'e, to Wilcox's sugar fields. The establishment of irrigation systems was a massive measure, enormously expensive, but it was key to increases in sugar yields. It made Grove Farm sugar a profitable crop. Ditch building, repair and rerouting would consume much of the plantation's activity throughout the next century.

Grove Farm also developed ditch systems that fed water from its lands and Lihue Plantation's

---

Top: Recognizing that termite infestation was destroying their housing stock, plantation management built Kaua'i's first hollow tile houses in April 1938. Grove Farm was also among the first plantations to develop housing that employees could own, replacing the old system in which sugar workers rented their homes from the plantations. Here, Mrs. Laureano Abines holds her son in front of their hollow tile home at Puhi, the first one built on the island.
Bottom: Grove Farm was famous for its housing innovations, not all of which caught on. This home, whose exterior walls were made of sheets of pressed sugar cane fiber called canec, was designed in 1936 by W.M. Moragne.

lands to Koloa Plantation, the water-deprived plantation on the south side of the Hā'upu Range from Grove Farm. Grove Farm also ran water across Koloa Plantation lands to the next plantation, McBryde Sugar Company. Eventually, a tunnel under the Hā'upu Range would feed water from Kū'ia Stream above Grove Farm's lands to Koloa Plantation's Waitā Reservoir, which had been built to increase the latter's irrigation capacity.

In addition to selling his irrigation design services, Wilcox supplemented his income in the early days by serving as tax collector and roads supervisor, another way of putting his engineering education to work.

Wilcox kept his own books in the early days, and some of those records survive, written in his loopy script. A company today would have lists of computer gear and office equipment, supplies and personnel costs. In that very different time, Wilcox's ledger wrote of a $14 cart repair, a pair of wood barrels for $4, saddle repairs for $3.75 and a new Mexican saddle for $14. He paid $10.50 for a half-dozen pickaxes, $30 for two dozen shovels, $1 for a load of firewood, $2.43 for eighty-one lbs. of salt and $0.50 for a quarter of mutton.

A tin of kerosene was $5, and a dozen gray wool shirts were $15. On Nov. 20, 1866, he paid $1 for some seeds for his garden. Wilcox apparently would entertain occasionally, and his liquor bill on Nov. 1, 1873, included $12 for a twelve-gallon barrel of ale, $12 for six bottles of brandy and $9 for six bottles of whiskey. A year earlier, on Nov. 22, 1872, he picked up a case of Norway beer for $9.50.

He lived in a wide, grass-thatched house near the rim of Nāwiliwili Valley. Within a short time, he built an office a short distance away. The house and the office, now with metal roofing, still stand on the grounds of Grove Farm Homestead Museum.

When the initial ditch proved successful but limited, Wilcox expanded the irrigation system. He also built a pump system to bring water up from Nāwiliwili Stream to a cistern at his house and office complex.

In 1870, Wilcox bought the land under Grove

"I had learn so much from Grove Farm."

Chick Cacabelos, 81, is a Grove Farm retiree and son of a Grove Farm retiree. He was born in House 403, Puhi Camp, to parents who immigrated from Ilocos Norte in the Philippines. He attended Lihue Grammar School, during summers between Kauai High School sessions he picked pineapple for Grove Farm and when he graduated he went to work for the company full time.

"Mr. Henry Oshima was my boss in the carpentry department. He suggested I also learn plumbing and welding. We would go back and forth between Puhi and Koloa Mill, doing welding and plumbing," he said.

During the Korean War, Cacabelos joined the Army, but never got to Korea. He did spend time at Fort Jackson in South Carolina and joined up with other servicemen to take trips to East Coast sights including New York City, Washington D.C. and the beaches of Florida. "I traveled a lot," he said.

Back at Grove Farm, he became a "dynamite man" at the Grove Farm quarry and in constructing tunnels. At tunnels, they would drill six-foot-deep holes in the rock and pack them with blasting caps and powder. In the early days they used fuses, and later battery-powered igniters. "We blew it out. Boom!"

He joked that former Grove Farm chief operating officer Allan Smith would say in mock awe, "You're a dynamite man. We don't want to mess around with you!"

During his forty-four years with Grove Farm, Cacabelos was also an equipment operator, running backhoes and bulldozers. In pineapple season, he was a truck driver. He is clearly proud of the diversity of his accomplishments.

"I had learn from the old-timers, and then my helpers, I teach them, too. I learn from the Filipinos, the Japanese, the Hawaiians, even the haoles, and I keep it in here," he said, pointing to his head.

"I tell you, I had learn so much from Grove Farm."

Avelardo "Manok" "Chick" Cacabelos

Farm from Widemann for $12,000, giving him title to the plantation he had managed and then leased for six years. Three-quarters of the purchase price was borrowed, but Wilcox was able to pay off the $9,000 in loans by 1874.

Wilcox bought other lands, and apparently not always because they made sensible additions to his plantation. In an oral history, Charles J. Fern, the longtime editor of *The Garden Island* newspaper, reports that some of his purchases may have been driven more by charity than a desire for land acquisition. He asked an interviewer, "Have you ever come across any records about how many times Mr. Wilcox bought some of these kuleanas around here? I'm sure he bought them many times over and got pleasure out of doing it, and we all know that he was a great one for wanting to help people in every way possible. He certainly helped churches of all faiths on the island. It didn't matter what the faith was."

Wilcox recognized both the bright future of sugar cane and the economies of scale, and expanded his land holdings, acquiring a twenty-five-year lease on the Haʻikū lands adjacent to his plantation.

He also recognized what the earliest sugar planters had not—that there were significant benefits to operating both the plantation that grew the sugar cane and the mill that ground and turned it into granular sugar. His first step was to seek a more equitable contract with the owners of the Lihue Mill, and when that didn't work, he decided to get his own mill.

In 1876, Wilcox sailed to Germany and then Scotland, and ultimately ordered his own milling equipment from Scotland. It was a steam-driven unit capable of milling all of Grove Farm's cane well into the future.

The loss of Grove Farm's cane would damage Lihue Mill's output, and Lihue Plantation chief Paul Isenberg made Wilcox an offer he could not refuse. He proposed giving Wilcox a better percentage of the mill's output from processing Grove Farm cane, and also offered to buy the new Scottish mill for use on sugar to be grown on Hanamāʻulu lands to the

Top: The old dining room in the main house at Grove Farm Homestead Museum holds a card table overseen by Kimo Wilder's painting of George N. Wilcox. The card table was built at Mid-Pacific Institute, to which Wilcox was a major early donor.
Above: Most of the main house at Grove Farm Homestead is one room wide, with broad verandas on both sides. It provided comfortable flow-through ventilation throughout the home.
Right: A 1915 two-story addition to the main house at Grove Farm Homestead was designed by Clinton B. Ripley, who also designed the Kauaʻi County Building.

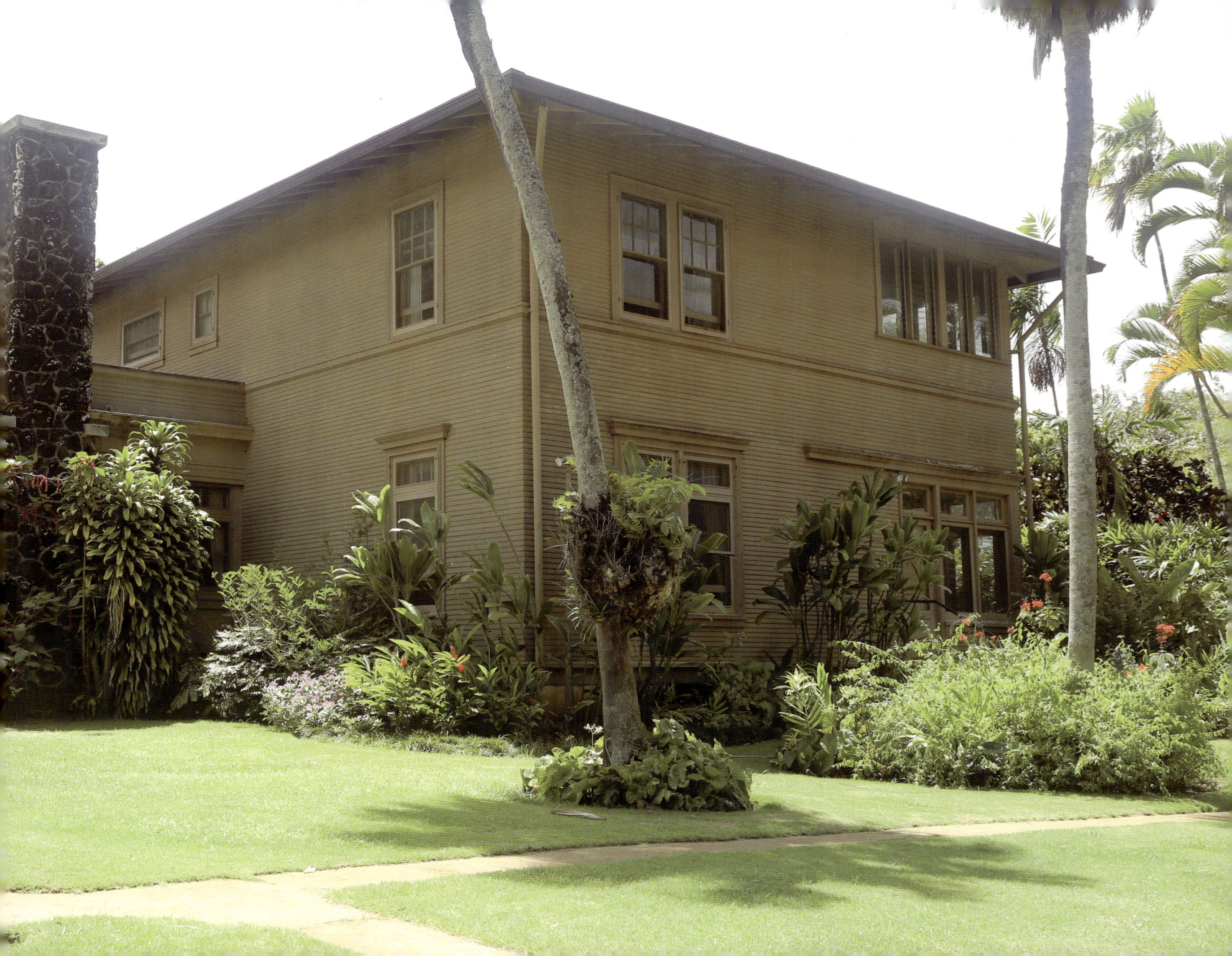

north of Lihue Plantation's core acreage. Wilcox accepted the proposal, with one additional proviso. Wilcox was deeply supportive of his family, and knew that his brother Albert was having trouble growing cane in the wet bottomlands of Hanalei. His deal with Isenberg included having Wilcox's brother, Albert, run the Hanamā'ulu Plantation that would supply cane to the new mill.

By now, Wilcox's brother, Sam, and his family had moved to Grove Farm to help him run the company. Wilcox built the first telephone line on the island, and only the second in the state, linking Grove Farm with the community doctor in Kōloa. He built it, according to the book *Grove Farm Plantation*, so that his sister-in-law, Emma, could check with the doctor when her new babies were ill. In 1880, Wilcox helped found a community telephone company.

As his sugar business grew, Wilcox recognized that he was at risk from inefficient suppliers, shippers and other operations that did business with his. He quickly began a series of investments, collaborations and partnerships that would protect Grove Farm. One of his first investments responded to inadequate shipping services to remote Kaua'i. He bought interest in one and then another interisland ship to ensure Kaua'i would get improved service.

Wilcox, at the urging of friends, ran for the national legislature and won in 1880—the same year his old mentor Hermann Widemann was defeated in his try for the legislature. Wilcox spent part of each year thereafter in Honolulu for the legislative sessions, deeply involved in Kingdom politics.

Grove Farm had fifty employees farming 1,200 acres by 1880, and needed more workers in order to expand its plantation. Early workers primarily included Hawaiians and Chinese laborers, but the supply of labor was tight. An early solution of the sugar planters was to find other Pacific Islanders who might fit readily into the Island community. Wilcox hired eighteen Gilbert Islanders, who the Hawaiians called Kilipakis. Their home nation is now known as Kiribati.

Housing was built for them and they were trained for working the irrigation, planting and harvesting systems on the island, but they appear not to have liked life in the Hawaiian chain. After five years, they went home.

Grove Farm joined other plantations in importing labor from a dizzying range of locales, and that mix of Japanese, Portuguese, Korean, Filipino and many other ethnicities would build the multicultural community that forms modern Hawai'i.

Left: *Grove Farm's headquarters, with its large safe on the right, is shown in 1934, the year it was built. Manager E.H.W. Broadbent's office and desk are visible in the small room at back.*
Right: *In 1943, a military band led by an accordion player provides the entertainment at a war bond rally fronting the Grove Farm office. Palm fronds festoon the stage area. Plantation-built grandstands are located on the left and right.*

12 GROVE FARM, KAUA'I: 150 Years of Stewardship and Innovation

In 1881, Princess Ruth Keʻelikōlani, the wealthy granddaughter of King Kamehameha I, sold Wilcox a 10,500-acre parcel at Haʻikū. It lay adjacent to land Wilcox already owned and included acreage he had been leasing. The princess reportedly made the sale in order to finance construction of a palace, Keōua Hale, which she completed in 1883 in Honolulu. Ruth Keʻelikōlani died that same year. She never lived in her palace, preferring her nearby thatched house, but she lay in state in the grand Victorian structure on her death.

Ruth Keʻelikōlani left her vast holdings—estimated at more than 350,000 acres on several islands, including Keōua Hale—to her niece, Bernice Pauahi Bishop, who did live in the house. Those lands formed the bulk of the property Bishop would use to endow the Bishop Estate/Kamehameha Schools on her own death in 1884.

Wilcox ran his growing empire from a two-room office building on the grounds of what is now Grove Farm Homestead Museum. The office still stands just across a landscaped area from the cottage where he slept. He had both dogs and cats. In the early days of the plantation, Wilcox famously rode his plantation on horseback, trailed by his pack of dogs. In those days, the dogs dozed on the office porch when Wilcox worked inside. Today, it is the descendants of his cats that sleep on the porch.

There's a story about someone approaching the office while Wilcox worked inside. The dogs would bark and Wilcox would call out, "Come on up. They never bit an honest man."

As a young man, Wilcox had hand-dug guano fertilizer—bird poop—on Jarvis Island. In that case, he was working for someone else, and the guano was headed for the U.S. East Coast. But he recognized that sugar cane was both a thirsty and a hungry crop, and that fertilization was needed to protect sugar cane yields. Wilcox, in 1890, became president of a new company, the North Pacific Phosphate and Fertilizer Company, which mined guano on Laysan Island, in the northwest Hawaiian Island chain.

Teams of workers, equipment, their housing gear and all other necessities were shipped to establish an operation to dig guano on Laysan, which lay 830 miles from Līhuʻe, and more than 900 miles from Honolulu. Seabird guano, from the Laysan albatross, booby and other nesting colonies on the island, is rich in nitrogen, phosphorus and potassium, nutrients desperately needed by the sugar crop of the Hawaiian Islands.

The guano business was not initially a profitable one, but Wilcox was confident in its future. In 1894, he and Paul Isenberg invested in a fertilizer processing facility in Kalihi on Oʻahu to improve the product and help it meet the requirements of

---

Left: Workers load cane in a Grove Farm field circa 1880. Oxen are hitched to carts that haul the cane to the Lihue Mill. Note supervisors on horseback. One of the toughest jobs on the plantation was hāpai kō, to carry cane. Workers shouldered loads of cane stalks up narrow planks before dropping them onto the carts; several of these planks are visible here.

Right: The Grove Farm office in the early 1880s looks much as it still does today. Here George Norton Wilcox did his daily bookwork, paid his employees and met with visitors. His dogs often slept on the porch as he worked inside. The building is now the office of the Grove Farm Homestead Museum.

"Gaylord Wilcox was the last of an era."

Carlina Tumbaga Vea, 81, arrived in the Islands from the Philippines in 1946 from the family home in Sinait, Ilocos Sur. Her father had gotten a job as an irrigator with Kekaha Sugar Company, and called for her mother and four kids to join him. They moved into a home in Mānā Camp, which no longer exists.

She was thirteen and attended Mānā School before going to Waimea High School and then to a nursing program on Oʻahu to become a licensed practical nurse. She worked at Wilcox Hospital for a year, then married and raised four children while working as a nurse at the Kauaʻi Veterans Memorial Hospital.

Her Grove Farm connection came as an offer to serve as a part-time nurse for Gaylord Parke Wilcox, the nephew of Grove Farm founder George N. Wilcox. Wilcox had been a vice president of American Factors, which was the owner of Lihue Plantation and Kekaha Sugar. When his uncle George died, the family turned to Gaylord to run Grove Farm.

Gaylord Wilcox was married to Ethel Kulamanu Mahelona and had built the manor known as Kilohana near the Grove Farm office. At the time Vea was asked to help, Gaylord's wife had died and Gaylord himself was suffering health issues.

It was a different time, and Gaylord Wilcox was the last of an era. He had a maid, a cleaning woman, the cook, a night nurse, a chauffeur, people working in the garden and other staff.

"He was lucid," Vea said. He continued to conduct Grove Farm business, often being visited to talk about the family company by president Sam Wilcox. He walked haltingly, with a cane. His meals were brought to him and when he needed to go somewhere, a chauffeur would drive. Vea was a nurse, but she said her duties were more of a secretary and companion.

"The chauffeur would drive. He (Gaylord Wilcox) would sit in the front and I would sit in the back. I remember going to the bank, the pharmacy. If he had a board meeting, we would go to the Grove Farm main house (now Grove Farm Homestead Museum). I remember I walked the whole yard while he was in the meeting."

She would sometimes write out checks for him to sign. "He was a fantastic stamp collector. The first check I wrote was for a stamp with an upside-down plane on it."

Caring for him was easy work since he did not require much skilled nursing, and she had ample free time.

"He said, 'You can read any book in my library as long as you put it back where it came from.' And I did. I had a book for upstairs and a book for downstairs. And I learned to play puzzles, jigsaw puzzles. He would do them and then put the date on them. They are hard puzzles and he had a lot of them."

Carlina Tumbaga Vea

---

sugar planters.

The challenges in finding labor for the sugar fields led to increasing mechanization. In 1888, Grove Farm took delivery of two massive Fowler steam plows, which would replace the use of oxen in plowing fields. The Fowlers worked in twos. They sat at each end of a field, linked by a cable that carried a double-ended plow. One engine would winch the plow across the field, both machines would roll forward, and then the other would winch it back. It was a complex process, but far faster than plowing by oxen. The cable plow cut through the ground at the breakneck speed of five miles per hour.

With Wilcox's earlier purchase of a Scottish steam mill and the Lihue Mill's own conversion to steam, Grove Farm was helping transform the energy landscape. The earliest mills and most agricultural activities in the early years were operated by animal and human power. That was changing with the advent of steam power, and would continue to change with the adoption of steam transportation, which included steam locomotives to replace oxcarts and the steady shift to steamships to replace sail-powered schooners.

Wilcox earlier had bought an interest in several schooners to assure access to shipping. In some cases, he did it to ensure good transport rather than because he thought it was a sound investment. He talked about it with historian Ethel Damon. His interviews with Damon are housed at Waioli

Corporation's Grove Farm Museum.

"(Capt.) Foster offered me an eighth share in the (schooner) *C.R. Bishop* and I took it, not because I thought it would ever pay, but because it was a good thing for the community to have a good vessel. and later, in 1885, he joined sugar growers Paul Isenberg, Henry P. Baldwin and Samuel Alexander in investing in the competing sugar processor, American Sugar Refining Company.

The two refineries, each backed by immense

When a monopoly threatened his financial interests, Wilcox fought it with his checkbook.

That is the way I have made a good many of my investments, first and last. When my brother Albert heard that I had an eighth share in her he said he wanted one too, so he went to Foster and asked him to sell him an eighth. Foster said all right. And the *C.R. Bishop* paid well—twenty-five percent—and first class passage to Honolulu was only $5 in those days," Wilcox said.

In 1883 he bought into the Inter-Island Steam Navigation Company. The firm competed in interisland shipping with Wilder Steamship Company, but they ultimately merged in 1905. The firm, in 1929, became the parent of Interisland Airways, which in turn became Hawaiian Airlines. Inter-Island Steam Navigation continued providing passenger service between the islands until 1947, after which air travel became essentially the only way for the general public to travel between the islands, and tugboat-hauled barges became the primary movers of cargo.

Wilcox was agnostic when it came to the issue of competitive businesses versus monopolies. When it suited his purpose and benefitted him, as with Inter-Island Steam Navigation, he was pleased to participate in a monopoly. But when it threatened his financial interests, he fought with his checkbook. As sugar baron Klaus Spreckels grew increasingly powerful in controlling the refining of Hawaiian sugar through Spreckels' California refinery, Wilcox participated in several attempts to keep competition alive. He and others shipped sugar around Cape Horn to the U.S. East Coast,

sugar fortunes, conducted ugly battles over the next decade. Both sold sugar below cost to try to control the market. Wilcox sold his interest at a thirty-three percent profit in 1888. The refinery wars continued with significant financial losses on both sides until the refineries determined that collaboration was the only answer. They began working together, although the power continued to shift back and forth.

Hawaiian sugar refinery wars ended in 1895 when American Sugar Refining bought out Spreckels' California refinery. Hawai'i's sugar companies in 1906 formed their own refinery in Crockett, California, under the name California and Hawaiian Sugar Company. That company still exists, but is now owned by non-Hawaiian interests. California and Hawaiian Sugar is now marketed by Domino Foods, a successor to American Sugar Refining.

The Kaua'i sugar companies, Grove Farm included, recognized that in an increasingly technical agricultural industry and a growing and complex economy, education was essential. Grove Farm launched an interest in funding education that straddles three centuries and that continues today. In 1890, George N. Wilcox joined the Smith and Rice families in forming a Malumalu School. It

---

Top: For protection from the cutting edges of sugar cane leaves and from the sun, field workers often wore far more clothing than might be expected in the subtropics. A Japanese field worker in protective gear carries her lunch in a kau kau tin.
Bottom: In May 1951, Pat Rapozo works a new mobile radio system at Grove Farm headquarters.

GROVE FARM, THE INNOVATOR 15

was also known as Kauai Industrial School, a three-story boarding facility on Grove Farm land above the Hulē'ia River valley. The school building was on Hulemalu Road, a quarter-mile east of the Puhi Road intersection. Teachers instructed between three and four dozen students in traditional book learning as well as trades, including woodworking, blacksmithing and farming.

Wilcox also contributed to education on O'ahu. In addition to backing his own alma mater, Punahou School, he was an early supporter when Mills Institute for Boys was established in 1892. Mills and the much older Kawaiaha'o Seminary for Girls shared a campus in Mānoa Valley starting in 1908. That year, George Wilcox donated $100,000 toward the school's endowment, adding to his already large regular donations. The two schools merged in 1922 and 1923 to form Mid-Pacific Institute. The schools were notable for the democratic approach to schooling. There were no ethnic or class restrictions on entrance. Students included members of Hawaiian royalty along with children of Japanese, Chinese, Korean and later Filipino immigrants, Caucasian plantation children and others.

G.N. Wilcox's charitable instincts were famous. In addition to the schools, he gave to the YMCA, the YWCA, the short-lived children's center Kaiaka Preventorium and the Salvation Army. He donated to his parents' employer, the Hawaiian Board, the successor to the American Board of Commissioners for Foreign Missions. But he also, very quietly, donated funds to help build Roman Catholic churches on Kaua'i.

And he was a soft touch on a personal basis. Any number of his employees and even non-employees in the community would tell of their generous friend "Keoki" or even "Georgie." Newspaper editor Charles J. Fern tells this story, partly in pidgin, with the Hawaiian words *hana hana* (work), *kōkua* (help) and *makuli* (sometimes written *makule*, meaning old). *Keoki* is the Hawaiian word for the name George.

"This is apropos of him and of his life…driving up the Nāwiliwili Hill, I picked up an old Chinaman as he was walking along and I asked him where he lived. He said, 'Down Halehaka Way,' and I said, 'You hana hana?' And he said, 'No, no hana hana.' And I said, 'Who kokua?' And he said, 'Makuli Georgie kokua.' He called him Georgie. He didn't call him Keoki. Of course, there was only one Makuli Georgie," Fern said.

Politically during the last decade of the 1800s, Hawai'i was in an uproar as Western business interests battled with King Kalākaua and on his death, his sister Queen Lili'uokalani, for power. George Wilcox had served in the House of Representatives from 1880 to 1887, when he was elected to the House of Nobles, the equivalent of the senate. He served there until 1892, a year when the queen's cabinet repeatedly formed and collapsed.

Charles T. Gulick replaced Charles Spencer as minister of the interior in September 1892, but Gulick lasted only fifty-seven days until the queen in November appointed George Wilcox her third minister of the interior in two months, and he managed to hold the post for only another two months. He was relieved of his post a few days before the overthrow of the Hawaiian Kingdom, and replaced with John F. Colburn, whose own term lasted just four days—through the overthrow of the monarchy.

It was a Tuesday in January— January 17, 1893— when the *U.S.S. Boston* landed marines in Honolulu and U.S. Minister John L. Stevens recognized a new government under Sanford Dole. Wilcox thereafter was elected to the senate of the new Republic of Hawai'i, a position he held through U.S. annexation in 1898. For much of that time, he served as chair of the Senate Education Committee.

The Ha'ikū lands along the northern edge of the Hā'upu Range were among the first properties acquired by G.N. Wilcox for Grove Farm. Roughly 2,700 acres of Ha'ikū were sold to Cumberland & Western Resources LLC.

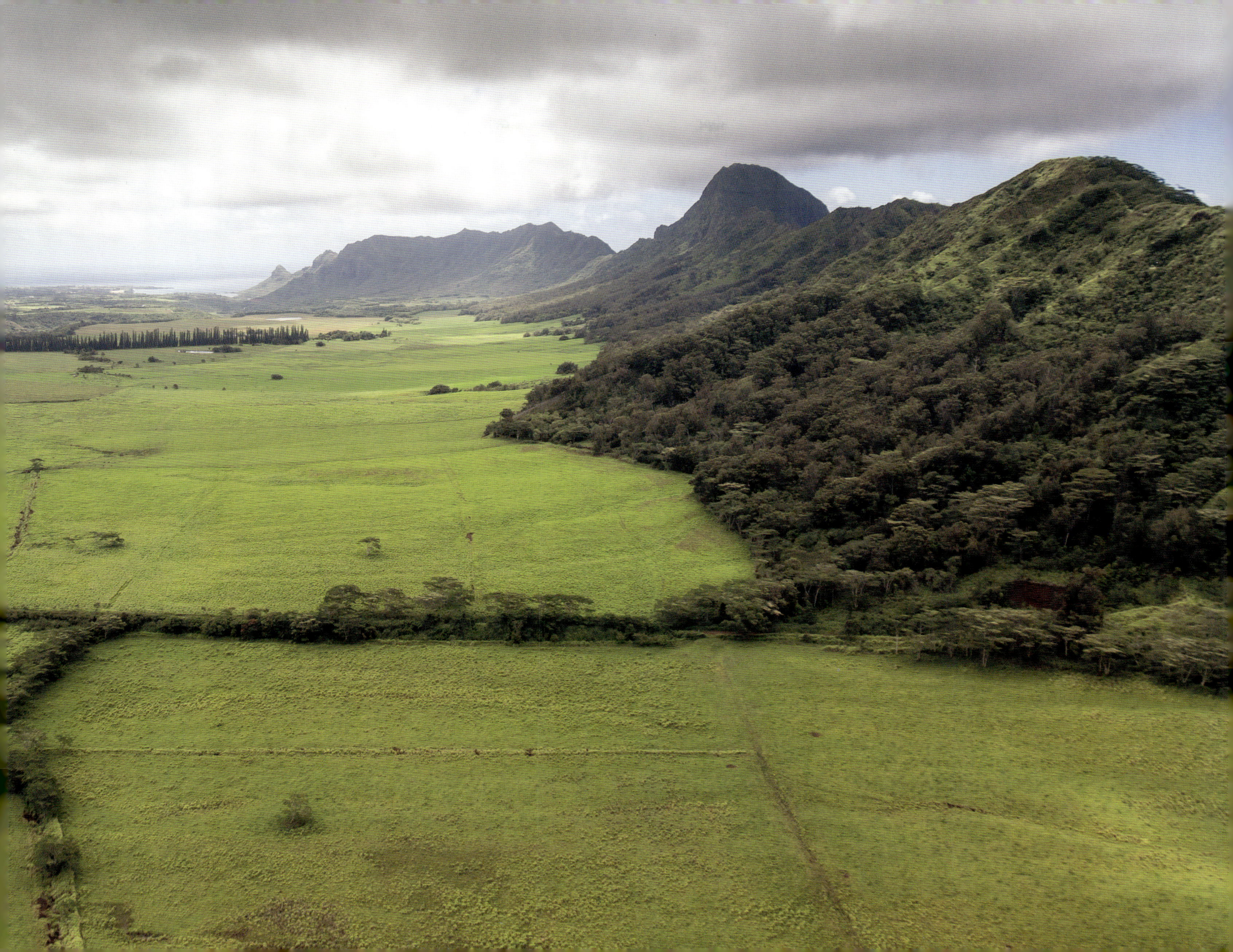

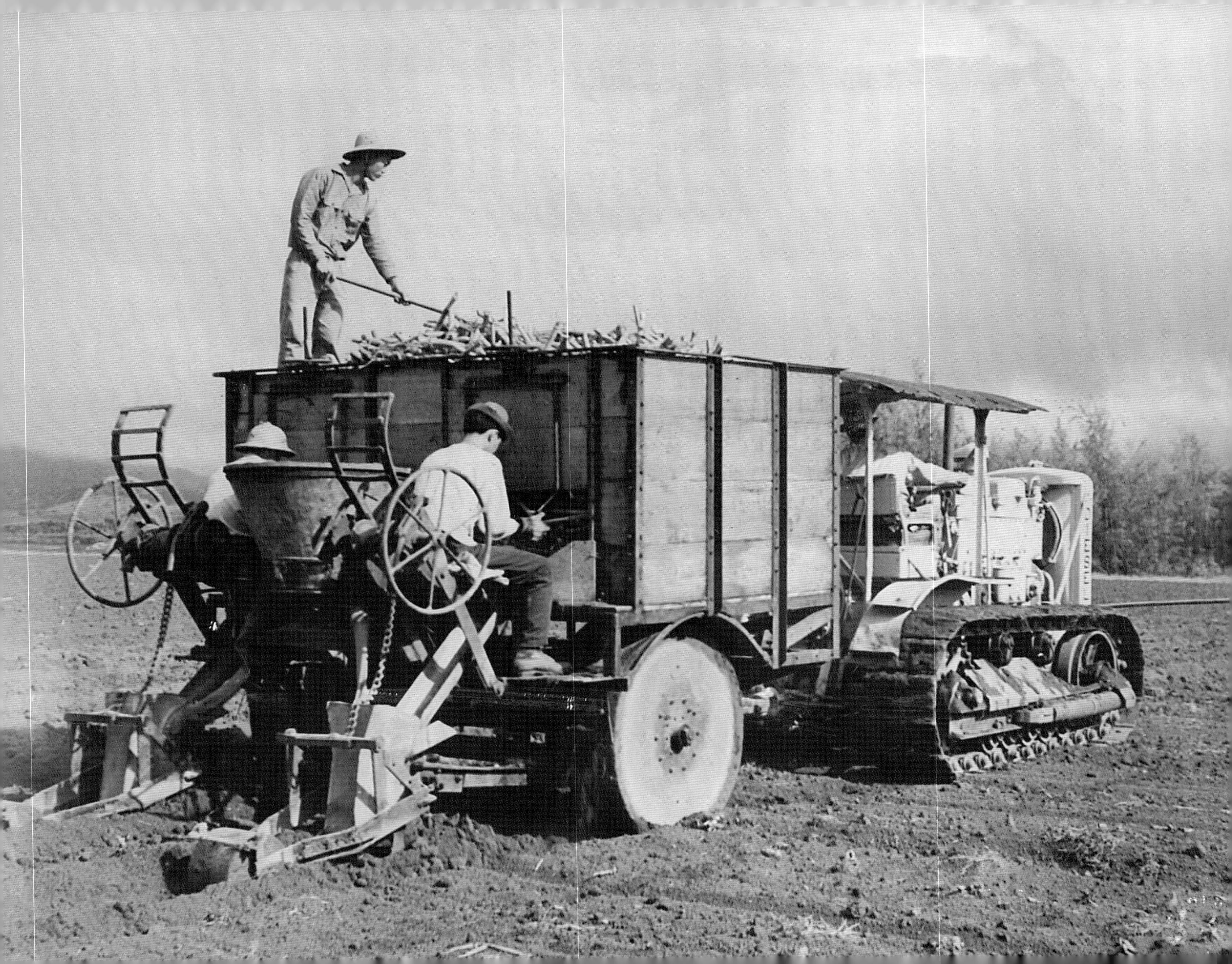

Wilcox was always on the lookout for talent, whether part of his family or not. He poached a New Zealand blacksmithing instructor from Malumalu School and put him to work at Grove Farm. He was E.H.W. "Ned" Broadbent. Broadbent started as a *luna*, or overseer, in 1894, and before long would be Wilcox's plantation manager and right-hand man. Broadbent's son-in-law, Dudley Pratt, was an attorney and would serve Grove Farm as its corporate counsel. Broadbent's grandson David W. Pratt would serve as Grove Farm president many years later, and would continue as a member of the Grove Farm board under the company's ownership by Steve Case.

Broadbent would continue Grove Farm's tradition of innovation, designing and building numerous pieces of sugar industry equipment that would be adopted throughout the territory. His Broadbent sugar cane planter went into production in 1920. The device was towed behind a tractor, had chutes that dropped cane sections into furrows, which were then covered with dirt by large disks and tamped down by rollers. The machine, using wheels recycled from an old Fordson tractor, could plant six acres a day with a tenth the manpower previously required.

As the plantation moved from oxcarts to steam-powered rail, Broadbent devised a way to use the excess steam to kill weeds that grew along the tracks. He developed a backpack fertilizer gun that allowed workers to easily deliver doses of fertilizer to cane-growing soil.

About 1918, after the First World War ended, Wilcox hired a young man with University of Hawai'i agricultural training. Aderial Hebard "Hib" Case was the son of Maui territorial judge Daniel Case. Hib Case had been born in Topeka, Kansas, in 1892, and had been raised on Maui where his father had been a county attorney in Wailuku before being named Maui County's territorial judge.

> **Wilcox poached a New Zealand blacksmithing instructor and put him to work at Grove Farm.**

Hib Case went away to Cornell for college, and then took farming courses at what would become the University of Hawai'i at Mānoa. After serving in the National Guard on O'ahu during the war, the twenty-six-year-old Hib Case was offered the Grove

---

Opposite: *A Grove Farm bulk planter, used from 1945 to 1947, permitted mechanized planting and fertilization of seed cane. Operated by four men, it could plant and cover 800 bags of seed cane—stalks of cane—per day. The bulk planter was designed by Grove Farm operations manager William M. Moragne and built in Grove Farm's shops.*
Above: *The first steamer to tie up to the new Pier 1 at Nāwiliwili Harbor was Inter-Island Steam Navigation Company's Hualalai, on July 22, 1930. G.N. Wilcox was instrumental in developing Nāwiliwili into an all-weather, deep-water port. Small fishing boats in the harbor celebrate the occasion with flags flying, while spectators in the foreground observe the proceedings from the Nāwiliwili jetty.*

Farm job. He would stay at Grove Farm his entire working career. Case started as a luna in the fields, and later became bookkeeper, office manager and eventually the company treasurer and chief financial officer. After he retired, he stayed connected as a trustee of the Wilcox Trust, which held a majority of the shares in the company.

He married Elizabeth McConnell, an Evanston, Illinois, girl who came to Hawaiʻi to teach school at the invitation of a friend who lived in the Islands. They had three sons: attorney Jim Case, sugar planter Bill Case and attorney Dan Case. The boys lived along Nāwiliwili Road, attending Lihue Grammar School and later Punahou School on Oʻahu.

"Those were all very happy memories," said Dan Case, Steve Case's father. "Our neighbors were the Alexander boys, sons of (later Grove Farm manager) W.P. Alexander, an agriculturist with experience in Cuba. We had a friend, Mike Fern, whose father, Charlie, ran *The Garden Island* newspaper.

"Sometimes Charlie Fern would hire a driver to take us kids around to Kōloa or Waimea Canyon. Sometimes we would stay at the Alexanders' mountain cabin in Kōkeʻe. We would spend a week in the summer at the YMCA program at Camp Naue in Haʻena.

"We lived next door to the manager's house, which was a playground for everybody. There was tennis, a swimming pool and a yard big enough for football. We hiked down in Nāwiliwili Valley. Papalinahoa had mangoes, massive Chinese and regular mangoes. We'd get mountain apples from the (Knudsen) Gap. The house was built by Digby Sloggett, and eventually, my dad lived in that house," he said. After Hib Case's death in 1965, managers Bill Moragne and Lyle Van Dreser would occupy the house.

Steve Case said he remembers that as a child, the family would visit his grandfather during summers and swim in the pool. Sometimes they stayed at Mabel Wilcox's cottage on Poʻipū Beach. "We'd spend five or six hours in the water, or hiking down by Māhāʻulepu."

Hib's son Dan Case's route back to Grove Farm was a fairly simple one. After graduating from Punahou in 1942, he attended college, served in the Navy and then went to law school. He was back in the Islands in 1952, and got work with a law firm headed by Dudley Pratt, who was married to the daughter of former Grove Farm manager E.H.W. Broadbent. Pratt eventually passed the Grove Farm legal services account on to Dan Case.

Back at the plantation, Wilcox, ever the innovator, was already an elderly man of sixty-eight in 1907 when he bought what some say was the first automobile on the island. It was an angular two-seater on tall wheels with a tiller for steering.

"I had the first automobile on Kauaʻi, you know. That was in 1907. It was a steam car, a motor car they called it... It was really a small steam engine burning gasoline, with a boiler. Yes, I drove it a little. But I soon gave it up," Wilcox said.

According to the account in the book *Grove Farm Plantation*, Wilcox didn't much like the steam-powered car. He preferred riding horseback, and did so well into his later life. But he understood the value of the new internal combustion vehicles. Within a few years, cars and trucks began appearing commonly on the island's roadways. Grove Farm acquired its first trucks with the purchase in 1915 of two Fords. The same year,

Top: View in 1951 of the Wilcox Tunnel's Haʻikū Portal, looking towards Kilohana.
Bottom: Grove Farm president Gaylord P. Wilcox displays a ti plant root, which was baked and used to produce a type of sugar called levulose, produced by Grove Farm from the 1940s to the 1960s. One of these plants is three years old, the other is seven.

Wilcox brought two tracked tractors to Grove Farm. They did well on steep terrain where steel-wheeled Fowler steam plows did not.

He was also actively looking for new crops for the island.

In 1905, Wilcox contributed funds to the Hawai'i Agricultural Experiment Station to conduct studies into tobacco and rubber as crops for the island. Wilcox was known to like a good cigar, and early reports indicated that tobacco did well in the Islands, although pest problems—notably cutworms, helped kill that crop as an industry. Rubber trees of the species *Manihot glaziovii*, commonly known as *ceara*, had been planted at Kōloa in 1893 and at Līhu'e, from seeds of the Kōloa stand, in 1899. The Līhu'e-area trees were in a gulch, growing on a swampy old taro patch. There were ceara plantations on other islands, and the experiment station conducted experiments in tapping the trees for their latex, which was made into rubber. An early experiment station report said, "The product, though very unattractive as it comes from the field, is capable of being turned into rubber of the first class without too great expense." But it was deemed inferior to the *hevea* rubber supplied from other parts of the world, and while there were exports from the Islands—notably from Maui—rubber did not develop into a lasting industry.

George Wilcox was interested in starch crops, like Hawaiian *pia* and *manioc*. He gave land around Līhu'e to a farmer named Wiebke for cultivation of pia or Polynesian arrowroot, *Tacca leontopetaloides*.

Wilcox said he enjoyed planting trees, and he did so both out of a personal interest in interesting new species, but also because of their value for conservation and economic benefit.

"When the crop was all in, the weeds out of the way, I always had the men plant trees. The first ironwood seeds I got was when W.O. Smith was sheriff and he planted some at the old courthouse. We planted all along the road up to Halehaka, but the roots got into the cane field and they had to come out," Wilcox said.

He recognized early the value of reforesting with trees for watershed enhancement. But also, wood was a valuable product, used for pieces of machinery, for house and bridge building, for firewood, for fence posts and for other uses.

"If I were to live another hundred years I would plant Norfolk pines. We think they are a valuable tree for posts and piles. Two or three years ago we took a number from the little grove at Halenanaha and drove them in as piles under the new chimney of Kekaha Mill. So that mill rests on a Grove Farm foundation," Wilcox said.

One of the issues for shipping goods into and out of Kaua'i was the lack of an all-season harbor. In the plantation's early days, ships anchored in Nāwiliwili Bay and cargo was brought by small boat or was floated to a pier on Kalapaki Beach. Equipment often fell overboard, and divers needed to recover them from the shallow bay. There was a small harbor in Hanamā'ulu Bay, but it was subject to large swells from the east.

In 1910, Wilcox began lobbying the Corps of Engineers to build a proper commercial harbor at Nāwiliwili Bay, which was coincidentally just

---

Top: *The Wilcox Tunnel through the Hā'upu Range is shown from the Kōloa side approach. The tunnel is twenty feet high and twenty feet wide. A railway was used to haul rock out of the tunnel during construction; an electric locomotive is visible at the tunnel entrance.*
Bottom: *In later years, virtually all Hawaiian sugar was marketed under the C&H label, but here in 1952, Grove Farm-grown Hawaiian Sunshine brand sugar is packaged in attractive five- and ten-pound bags for household use.*

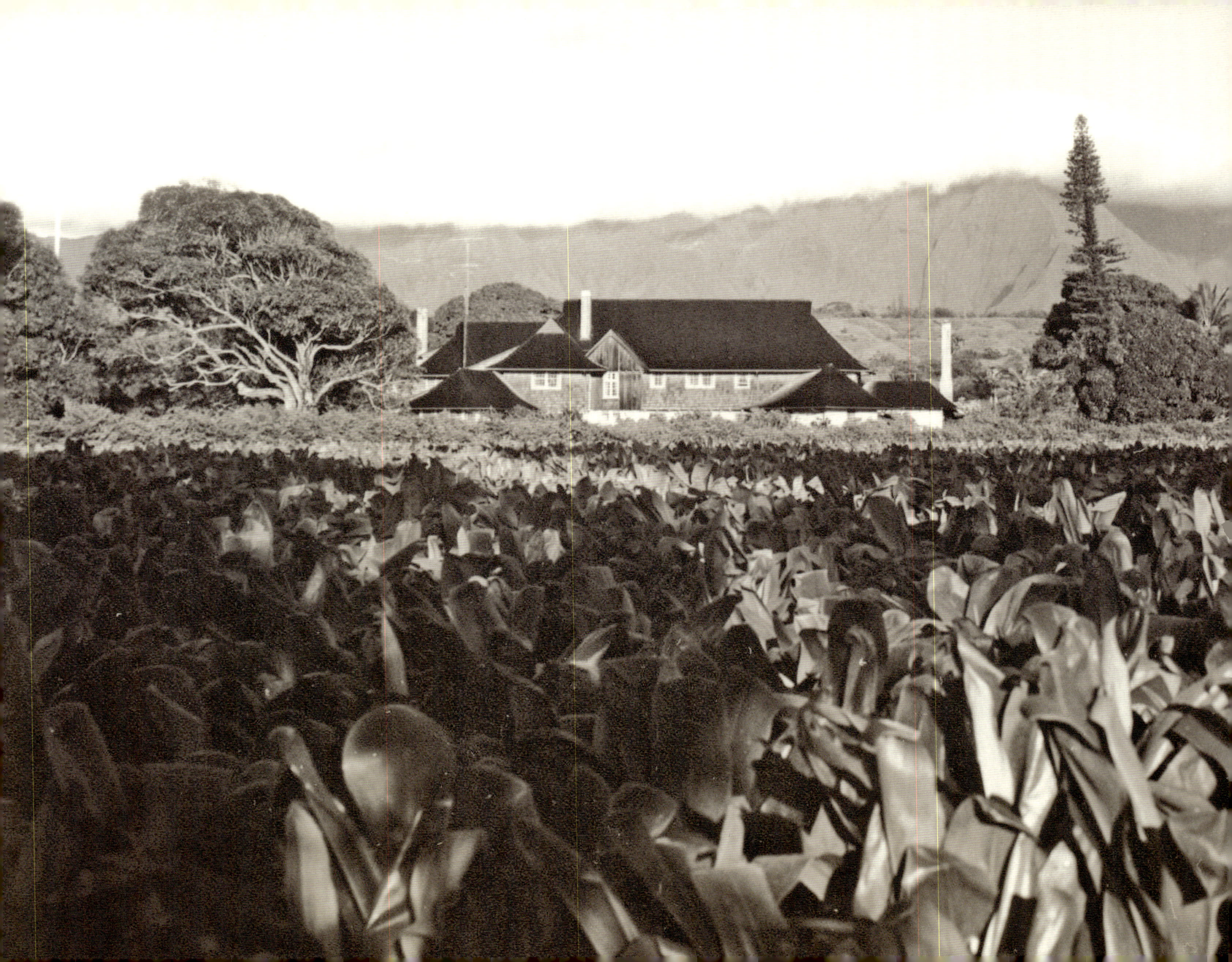

In 1953, Grove Farm grew ti plants in several locations, including the grounds of Kilohana, the home built for then-company president Gaylord P. Wilcox. The house is visible at left.

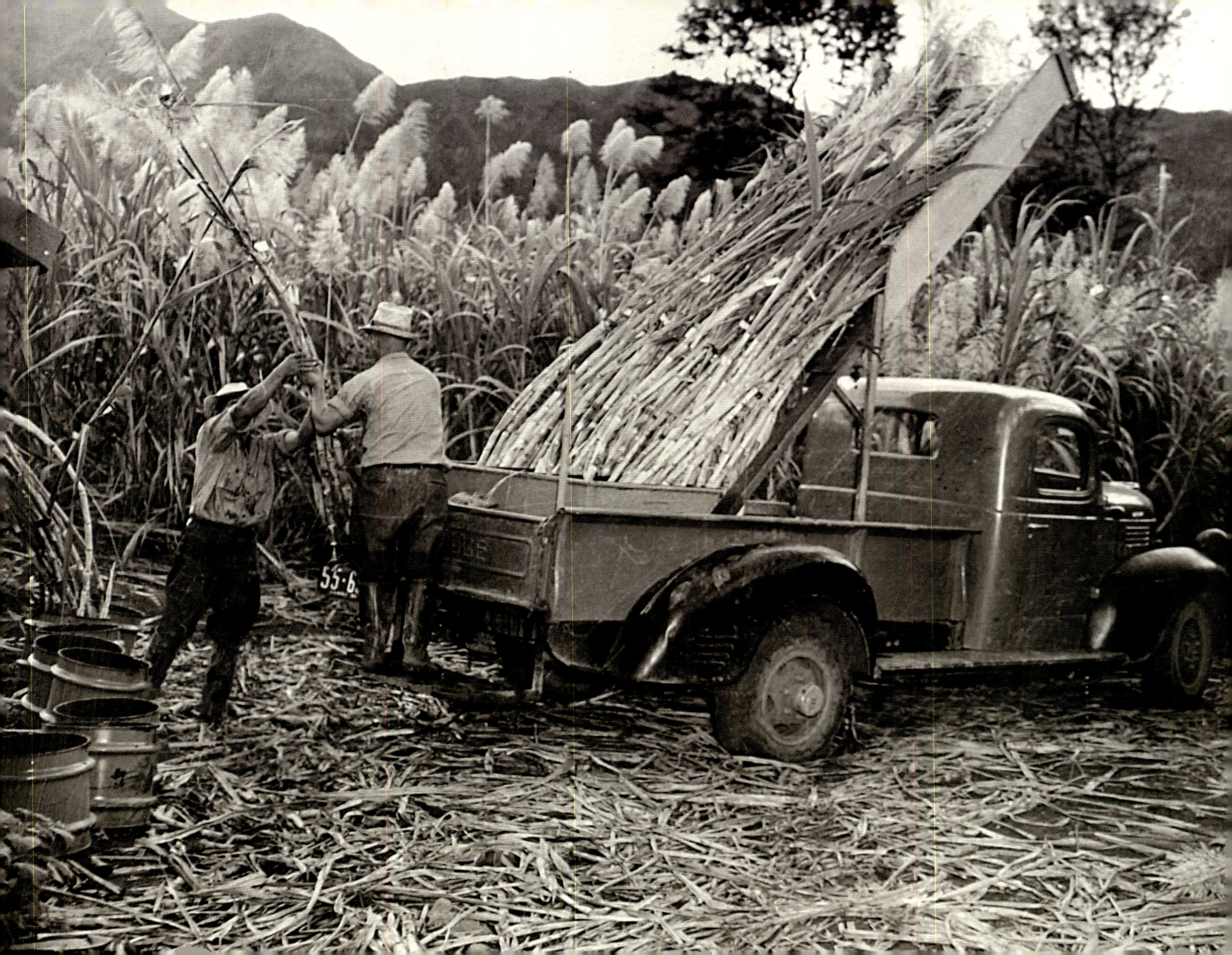

down the hill from Wilcox's headquarters and his plantation.

Wilcox made his case compellingly: "The harbor at Nāwiliwili is the only natural one on the island of Kauaʻi. It lies midway between the northern and the southern parts of the island and is the nearest point of departure both for Honolulu and California. Moreover, it is the port of call of greatest benefit to all the people of the island. It does not favor any one community, but is so centrally situated that it seems to have been intended by nature for the harbor of this island."

Getting the harbor built was a long process, and there was some opposition from interests promoting other locations. A breakwater was launched across a reef fronting the bay in 1926, and when the project ran out of money, Wilcox, by then eighty-eight years old, finished the breakwater out of his own pocket.

Meanwhile, the Wilcox stamp was all over Kauaʻi sugar operations. George's nephew Charles ran Koloa Plantation; brother Albert had run Lihue Plantation's Hanamāʻulu operations; and nephew Gaylord ran Makee Plantation, which would later become part of Lihue Plantation.

George N. Wilcox never married, but his siblings and their offspring played significant roles at Grove Farm. Brother Sam lived at Grove Farm and worked with his brother for most of his adult life. In 1922, George converted his plantation from a sole proprietorship to a corporation, distributing nearly half the stock to nieces, nephews and their children, and retaining a bare majority himself, to be voted in trust on his death by Sam's offspring: Etta, Elsie, Gaylord and Mabel. On their death, that portion of the company would also be distributed to the descendants of Abner and Lucy Wilcox.

Despite the increasing complexity of business, Wilcox kept a simple set of books: what went out, subtracted from what had come in. He

Left: In 1949, a truck is loaded with sugar cane with tassels. The energy used in sugar cane's flowering, or "tasseling," reduced sugar yields. But in the industry's early years, tassel production wasn't preventable. Later, chemical sprays would control tasseling, and cane with waving tassels was rarely seen.
Above: Safe from the office of G.N. Wilcox's Grove Farm Homestead office, now on display at the Grove Farm Homestead Museum.
Right: An old Grove Farm locomotive bell has been repurposed as a yard bell at Grove Farm Homestead Museum. The bell, now welded to an old truck wheel hub, was used to summon people for meals and telephone calls.

GROVE FARM, THE INNOVATOR 25

didn't borrow much, and he didn't distinguish for bookkeeping purposes between capital and operating expenses. Eventually, the man who kept his books had to keep two sets: one to meet government requirements and one for Wilcox's own satisfaction.

Office manager and later chief financial officer Hib Case recalls: "We kept, technically, two sets of books. One was the normal regular book that we kept mainly because of the United States income tax. The other set that we kept was just the expenditures during the year. When it would get to the end of the year, he'd say, 'How much do we have on the first day of January and how much have we got now?' So far as he was concerned, that was the profit we made for the year."

George Norton Wilcox died in January 1933, prompting a series of changes in the organization of his sugar company. Broadbent, plantation manager of Grove Farm for a generation, retired in 1936, and the reins were turned over to his assistant manager, William P. Alexander. Gaylord Parke Wilcox left his position at American Factors and moved to Kaua'i to run the family company, building a grand home at Kilohana. Hib Case, who had long been Wilcox's bookkeeper and office manager, became treasurer of the corporation in 1938.

The plantation was having difficulty finding labor, and this encouraged Grove Farm's managers and engineers to develop ways to do the work more efficiently. The coming of World War II increased the need for laborsaving devices, since many plantation workers were called up into the war effort. The plantation developed herbicide spray equipment to overcome the lack of workers to manually weed. The Grove Farm staff developed mechanized harvesting systems to replace the old hāpai kō ("carry cane") positions in which men

Left: The construction of the Wilcox Tunnel, which allowed truck traffic under the Hā'upu Range, employed a surplus World War II drilling rig. The tunnel was completed in April 1949. Pictured with the tunnel crew are civil engineer Elbert T. Gillin, tunnel superintendent C. Peterson and Grove Farm operations manager William M. Moragne.
Right: E.H.W. Broadbent was hired by G.N. Wilcox in 1895 and named Grove Farm's manager in 1902. A blacksmith from New Zealand and a noted inventor of agricultural equipment, Broadbent went on to run the company through some of its most successful years. He retired in 1936.

manually filled railcars with cane.

The plantation also continued its practice of studying alternative crops. In 1939, Grove Farm went into the pineapple business with a fifty-acre test plot. Over time, the company became a pineapple as well as a sugar company, finding that there were agricultural benefits in soil fertility and pest control to alternating the crops.

Grove Farm grew pineapple, but never had a processing facility. At various times, it sold fruit to each of the island's three canneries. The initial crop from fifty acres was consigned to Hawaiian Fruit Packers, but the firm's insistence that fruit be delivered in labor-costly small boxes instead of in bulk soured Grove Farm on the arrangement. Grove Farm, after all, prided itself on efficiency and labor-saving. A labor-intensive form of pineapple packaging ran against the grain.

The company next signed with Kauai Pineapple Co. That 1945 contract called for 150 acres of crop. Grove Farm used its extensive engineering expertise to mechanize its harvesting as much as possible—building its own machines to its own designs. Jack Larsen, in his 2010 history of key figures in the pineapple industry, *Hawaiian Pineapple Entrepreneurs*, said Grove Farm was "at the cutting edge of the industry in mechanical harvesting."

The company varied its acreage, never exceeding the 1953 total of 654 aces. Its highest production came in 1953 and 1954, when it produced more than 18,000 tons each year. By that time it was supplying two canneries: Kauai Pine and Hawaiian Canneries. The closing of both those canneries in 1962 ended Grove Farm's venture of more than two decades in pineapple farming. Some of the island's other sugar plantations also grew pineapple.

Other crops would join the cane and pineapple for Grove Farm. During World War I, the company turned over some of its fields to the war effort, growing tons of corn, beans and potatoes. In World War II, it did so again.

In 1936, Grove Farm planted a small plantation of lychee trees in Halehaka Valley. The fruit with its red skin and sweet white flesh was established from grafts taken from a tree in manager Bill Moragne's yard. Grove Farm ran the lychee farm for several years.

Left: *In 1940 Alejandro Rabago and Noboru Sasaki operate a Hillman blasthole rig at the Grove Farm blue rock quarry.*
Right: *Grove Farm engineer W.M. Moragne designed the Moragne Seed Cutter. Here in 1947, the planter designed by E.H.W. Broadbent sits in place under the seed cutter. Both units were built in the Grove Farm shop.*

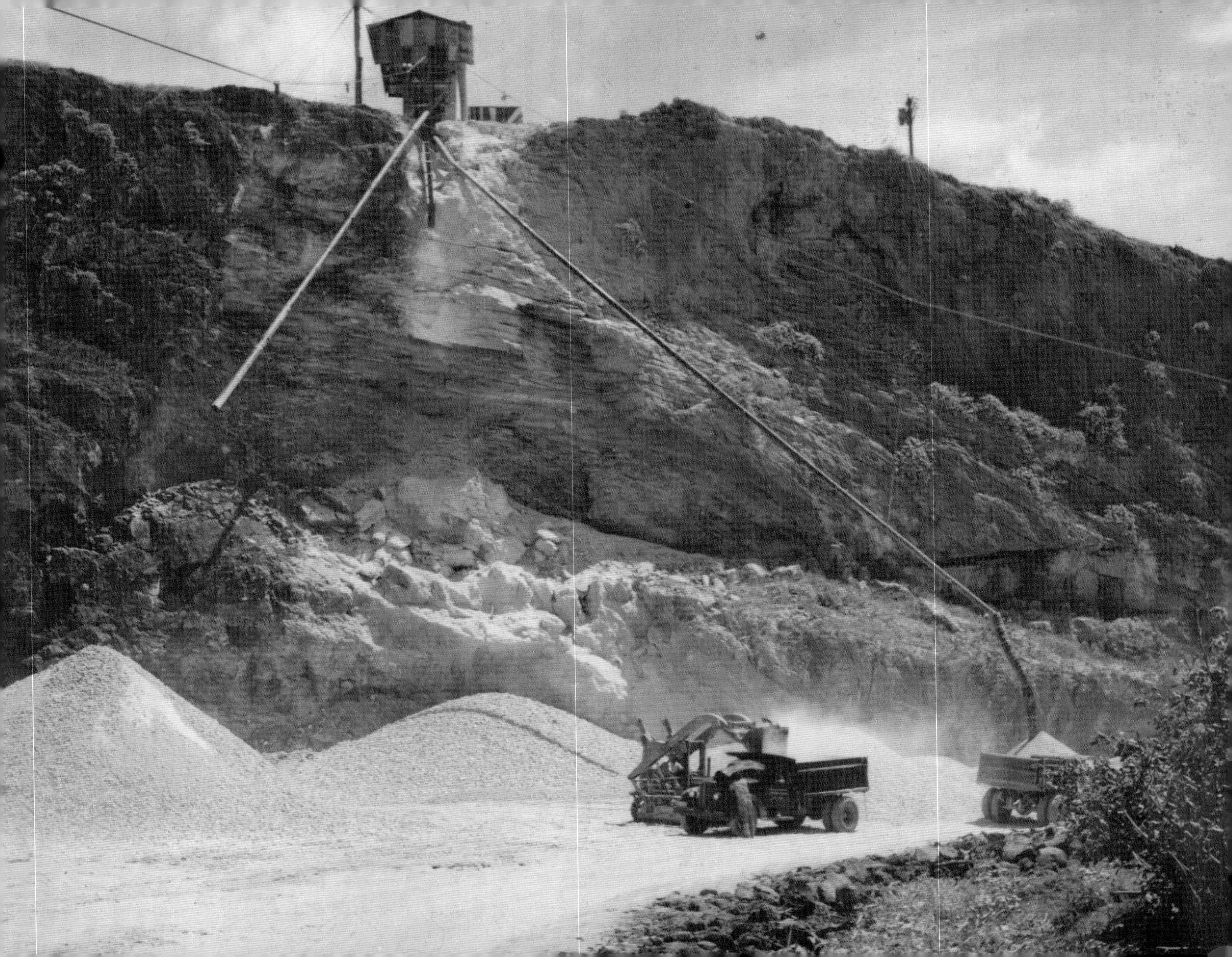

In the mid-50s, the company began planting ti (*Cordyline terminalis*) for production of a kind of sugar called levulose. Early Hawaiians knew that baked ti root created a sweet confection, and it turned out that the sweetness came from a kind of sugar different from cane sugar. Levulose provided sweetness, but could be eaten by individuals with medical conditions that proscribed cane sugar and it was used in medical applications.

For more than a decade, shiny green ti leaves waved over much of Grove Farm's land. Fields were growing in front of the Gaylord Wilcox Kilohana mansion, at the southeast corner of the intersection between Kaumuali'i Highway and Kīpū Road and elsewhere.

Former Grove Farm mechanic David Nobriga recalls that his machine shop built a ti harvesting machine, a big specialized plough that was pulled by a tractor. It had been designed by plantation manager Moragne, a gifted engineer.

Chemist Leonard Britton conducted extensive research into producing high-quality levulose. Britton apparently also ran a small still, converting the ti sugar into alcohol. Grove Farm programmer Michiye Funaku recalls that the chemist would occasionally drop by the Grove Farm headquarters with a bottle of *okolehao*—liquor distilled from the ti root sugar.

But the levulose project ultimately was called off when Grove Farm concluded it could not see the ti sugar operation becoming profitable without a much larger investment than Grove Farm felt it could afford.

Moragne wrote then: "Our operating costs have been substantially above our income and there does not appear to be an improvement in sight...we could not afford to underwrite additional losses which would be involved until the levulose program could be expanded to the point where profits were possible."

After the levulose project was closed, there were some discussions with Hawaiian ti root liquor manufacturer Ti Root Okolehau Hawaii Inc., as well as with several Mainland drug companies, but ultimately most of the ti plantation was plowed

Above: *In 1952, a tractor operator takes a steep ride on a pile of crushed rock at Grove Farm's hot mix plant.*
Left: *A Grove Farm sugar worker inspects a spray rig hooked up to a D4 tractor in 1947.*
Opposite: *High-grade crushed limestone is loaded into a customer's truck at Grove Farm's newly built limestone crushing plant in 1952. Limestone filler and mineral aggregate are dropped from crusher chutes above into separate piles for loading.*

under. For a time, a few acres were leased to an entrepreneur who cut blocks of ti trunk and sold them for houseplants, since they readily sprouted shiny, dark green leaves.

A Grove Farm rock crusher was enlisted into the war effort, supplying gravel for local airfields. Grove Farm's senior personnel were drawn into the war effort, too. Treasurer Hib Case became the island-wide food administrator. Engineer Bill Moragne was assistant director of the Office of Civil Defense.

During and immediately after the war there were investigations into mineral deposits on Kaua'i, which raised the possibility of mining. One of the most interesting projects, due to its strategic importance, was bauxite, the ore from which aluminum is derived. A territory-wide survey in which Grove Farm participated found that Kaua'i had some of the most favorable deposits.

When the war ended, some of the labor shortages eased, but unionization increased costs. Grove Farm was a small plantation, by Hawaiian sugar industry standards, and was unable to gain economies of scale with the roughly 3,000 acres it farmed. It also suffered from not controlling its own processing, since it continued to have its cane milled by the Lihue Plantation factory, Lihue Mill.

Alexander and his staff began looking at neighboring Koloa Plantation, which farmed nearly 3,780 acres, but had a mill. By combining the plantations, the company felt it could solve several problems—gaining economies of scale and also gaining control over its processing.

"Since Gaylord's time, Grove Farm always wanted a mill. When Amfac put Koloa Plantation up for sale, they assumed McBryde would buy it," said David W. Pratt, who would later manage Grove Farm. "I think it was kind of a surprise that it went to Grove Farm."

President Gaylord Wilcox and manager Alexander sold the concept of a takeover of Koloa to the majority of his stockholders with the help of his office manager Case and assistant manager Moragne.

The next problem—and one of the reasons Grove Farm hadn't been considered the first choice to take over Koloa—was that the two plantations were separated by the Hā'upu mountain range. Moragne devised a plan to tunnel a road through the mountain using surplus World War II gear that had been used by the military to dig munitions tunnels and air raid shelters. Grove Farm bought Koloa Plantation and its mill, and by summer of 1949 the tunnel was complete, linking the two plantations.

Despite its involvement with alternative crops, sugar remained the mainstay at Grove Farm. In 1963, the company leased an additional 900 acres from the Eric Knudsen Estate to expand its sugar farming. And by 1964, when the company was 100 years old, it had paid off the cost of the Koloa Plantation purchase, the cost of upgrading the mill to handle the additional cane processing capacity, as well as the extensive capital improvements projects required to bring the two plantations into a single functioning unit.

The plantation had long been in the housing

Right: George Norton Wilcox hated to be fussed over and usually arranged to be away from the Islands on his birthday to avoid the celebration. In 1931, however, he remained at home and was feted with a cake.
Below: Members of a weed spray crew pose with the tools of their trade in 1940.

business as well as the sugar business. As most plantations did, Grove Farm provided for many of the needs of its employees, including giving them places to live. From its earliest days, the company built housing for its employees in locations spread around the island so the workers could be close to the fields in which they labored. There were camps around the original company headquarters along Nāwiliwili Valley, at Halehaka Valley, A'akukui, near Halfway Bridge and eventually near the new company headquarters at Puhi.

After noting that termites were feasting on untreated house timber, Grove Farm began using termite-resistant concrete blocks for construction. It was one of the territory's leaders in using concrete for housing. As transportation systems improved, the company began focusing its housing effort to the Puhi area, near the company's new headquarters.

For most of the plantation's history, housing was provided for rent. But in 1955, Grove Farm launched an innovative program of home ownership for its workers. It was the beginning of a long history of Grove Farm building housing for the working class people on the island. Initially, its subdivisions were focused on its workers only, but later it sold lots and house-and-lot packages to the general public.

Hawaiian sugar was a powerful and lucrative industry for its first century, but after World War II, the industry began feeling the pain of rising costs and sugar prices that were not keeping pace. In the 1960s, many sugar firms lost money in their weaker years. That was particularly the case for plantations on the windward, rainier sides of the Islands. Sugar was a crop that liked sunshine, and cloudy days hurt yields.

Top: *Designed by W.M. Moragne and built by Grove Farm crews, the blue rock quarry and crushing plant operation is shown in 1949. The quarry was started the day after the Dec. 7, 1941 attack on Pearl Harbor, and for its first three years, much of the product was delivered to the armed services. The operation was later expanded to sell rock commercially.*
Left: *Inside the blue rock crushing plant in 1949: Telesforo Thomas, Sam Napoleon and Masaru Sasaki.*

GROVE FARM, THE INNOVATOR

While plantations on the sunny leeward sides of islands could get sugar tonnages in the double figures per acre, Grove Farm and others on the windward sides struggled to get eight or nine tons per acre. Grove Farm had gotten a twenty-year profitable run from its acquisition of Koloa Plantation, and its leaders considered another acquisition in hopes of gaining another leg-up on rising costs. Neighboring McBryde Sugar Company, an Alexander & Baldwin company, was the target, but despite extended study by both companies, they dropped discussions at the end of 1968. Several years later, that negotiation was reversed, and McBryde ended up leasing two-thirds of Grove Farm's land.

During the late 1960s, the company continued to work hard at finding innovative ways to make money off its crops. One proposal was to use excess bagasse—the fibrous material left after the sweet juice was ground out of cane stalks—to make xylose. Xylose is a sugar that can be manufactured from woody plant fibers. In May 1969, Grove Farm decided it did not make sense to proceed with building a xylose processing plant. It did consider for a time selling its bagasse to another firm that might be interested in financing and building a xylose plant, but ultimately nothing came of this.

In 1970, with the financial crisis for Grove Farm growing, Grove Farm's directors were looking into selling land at Māhā'ulepu for development. Selling land was anathema for a farming company like Grove Farm, but times were critical.

By 1972, it was even clearer that something had to be done. Grove Farm was struggling financially, and the latest proposals considered the unthinkable: If Grove Farm could not acquire another plantation, it might consider going out of sugar altogether. They were painful discussions for a family-owned company that had been nimble and imaginative enough to remain in a single dominant business for nearly 110 years.

As Grove Farm's historic departure from sugar farming was under discussion, the last surviving child of George Norton Wilcox's siblings, his niece, Mabel Wilcox, set out to preserve his legacy. She put into place Grove Farm Homestead Museum.

She had always lived on the old plantation headquarters estate, and she continued to roam the ancient home among the old books, and koa bowls and *lauhala* mats and artifacts. Using her personal financial assets, she bought from Grove Farm the original plantation headquarters, including George's office, his cottage, the main house where Wilcoxes had lived for more than a century, and the small plantation camp where workers lived. It included the duck pens and the pigs, the descendants of George N. Wilcox's cats, and the many species of trees he had collected and planted.

She created and funded the museum's endowment. Historian Barnes Riznik was hired as the museum's first director, and set up the sprawling historic property. He was succeeded by Bob Schleck, who had been one of Mabel Wilcox's early employees on the museum project. Mabel Wilcox would die in 1978 at the age of ninety-six.

Mabel Wilcox's creation preserved the early portion of Grove Farm's story, but Grove Farm itself would continue as a vibrant part of the economy of the island. If anything, as it moved out of agriculture, Grove Farm became a more complex venture as well as one more directly impacted by economic factors within and outside the state of Hawai'i.

Continuing the company's long tradition of support for education, under president Sam Wilcox's leadership Grove Farm donated 200 acres to the University of Hawai'i to create a campus for Kaua'i Community College. The acreage lay immediately across Kaumuali'i Highway from the company's Puhi headquarters, just on the outskirts of Līhu'e. To help sell the donation to his shareholders, Wilcox argued that it would not only be a boon to education on the island, but it would help increase the value of Grove Farm's surrounding lands.

That was important as Grove Farm's sugar era came to an end. ❦

Above: In 1951 a road crew grades and widens the roadway from the Puhi Shops to the Hulē'ia Bridge.
Opposite: A view of the working end of the Grove Farm, or Broadbent, Planter. The men riding the planter are feeding stalks of seed cane down chutes into furrows in the field. The rollers cover the seed cane and compact the soil.

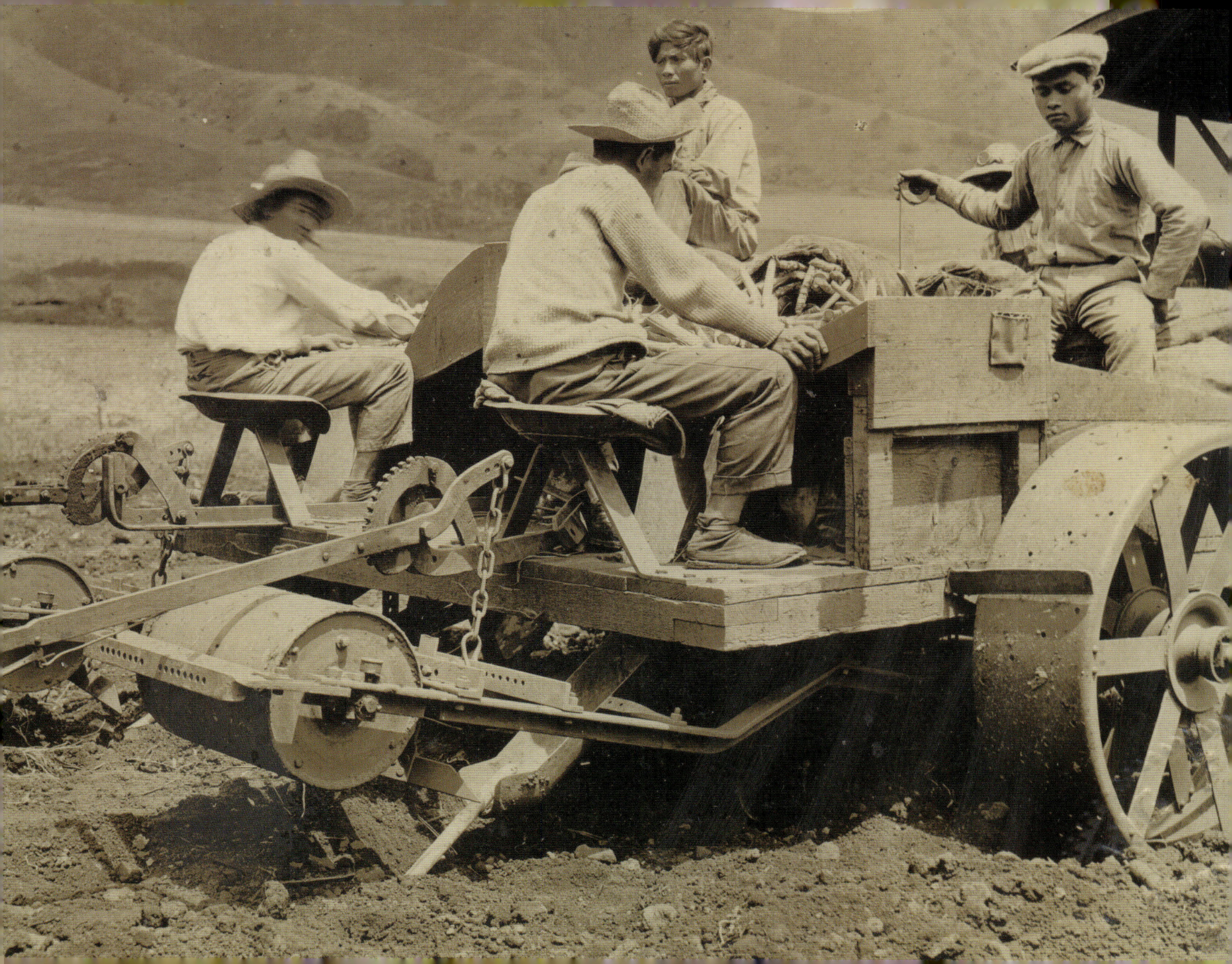

The Koloa Sugar Company mill, under construction in 1913 by Honolulu Iron Works.

Chapter 2
Koloa Plantation

"Businesses do play a critical role in developing and sustaining and sometimes reinventing communities."
—Steve Case

"Water sold to Kōloa started in early Kōloa history. This is the water that came from the Kūʻia Stream using the ditch through the Kōloa Gap. It is still in existence up there, but not used, of course, but you can see the outlines showing where it went… Kōloa was pretty hard up for water always and that was a big help to get Grove Farm's water."
—Gaylord P. Wilcox

Grove Farm's acquisition of Koloa Plantation in 1948 connected it to the earliest days of Hawaiian sugar. Like Grove Farm itself, Koloa had been a pioneer of the industry, bringing a series of new features to the growing and processing of the sweet grass.

Polynesians had long grown sugar cane, but it was not processed into granular sugar in the Islands until a Chinese sugar maker, Wong Tze-Chun, landed a mill and boiling pans on Lāna'i in 1802. He presumably used sugar grown by Hawaiians on the island. He packed up and returned to China after a single season.

A few other small operators bought locally grown cane and processed it. The planter Don Francisco de Paula Marin reported making granular sugar in 1819, and an Italian immigrant in Honolulu did so in 1823. Two Chinese entrepreneurs, Ahung and Atai, had a small plantation and a mill on Maui at Wailuku. Their operation, Hungtai, was the first record of bringing the farming and the processing of cane under one ownership. They were a vertically integrated company; they grew the cane, grounded it and processed it into white sugar and marketed the sugar through their store in downtown Honolulu. It is not clear whether they ever grew more than a few hundred acres of cane.

In his centennial book, *Koloa Plantation 1835-1935*, Arthur C. Alexander notes that sugar and molasses were being produced in Kōloa well before the plantation started. A Chinese sugar operator, presumably using the same Chinese expertise that Wong Tze-Chun possessed, had both granite and wooden mills for separating the juice from the fiber of the sugar cane. His operation was near the Kōloa mission station, and there was reportedly another not far away at Māhā'ulepu and a third sugar mill on the Tobey Plantation on Waihohonu Stream.

In 1833, the sailing ship *Hellespont* landed several Americans in Hawai'i. Peter Allan Brinsmade and William Ladd were both from Maine and were married to sisters who arrived with them. A single man, William Hooper, from Boston, was in partnership with Ladd and Brinsmade. They started a mercantile business in Honolulu, but felt agriculture was the future and leased land from King Kamehameha III. They acquired a three-acre site by a Kōloa waterfall for a mill site, and another 980 acres for the plantation.

In 1835, Ladd & Co. launched the first large-scale sugar plantation in the Islands. The initial efforts were problematic. There were labor issues, and also regular battles with the island governor, Kaikioewa. The initial mill, made of logs set vertically like Chinese stone mills, did not function well and wore out quickly. There was a shortage of cash—in that time, Hawai'i used a whole array of international coins for commerce—and Ladd & Co. paid workers in printed pasteboard cards known as "Kauai Currency." The thatched roof on the boiling house caught fire. A storm washed out the mill pond dam. They were drying sugar in the sun after "curing" it with clay obtained from Māhā'ulepu, three miles away. Manager Hooper was convinced that sugar could be a profitable venture, but in practice it wasn't going well. But Hooper persisted. In one of his greatest inventions, he ordered iron mill rollers and set them up horizontally instead

Top: The Waitā Reservoir was started in 1905 by Koloa Plantation manager Patrick McLane on the old Kōloa Marsh. The reservoir, one of the state's largest, allowed Koloa Plantation to expand sugar cultivation to dry lands at Pa'a and Weliweli. First built at a relatively small 300,00 gallons, it was expanded over the years, including a three-foot increase in dam height in 1931, which brought its capacity to 2.3 billion gallons and eventually covered the Hauiki and M&M Reservoirs.

Bottom: Livestock is run back and forth over layers of soil to compact the dam.

of vertically as all previous sugar mills had been assembled. They were established with two rollers below and one riding above them, the shafts bolted to wooden posts. He already had a dam, waterfall and waterwheel, and he hooked them together. The mill rollers were turned by gears on the water wheel shaft. It was the first iron sugar mill in the Islands and the first horizontal axis mill, and it transformed sugar processing. Horizontal mills could be fed automatically, the cane stalks slid to them, while vertical mills needed to be constantly hand-fed at great risk to the people feeding them.

If you simply boil down sugar juice, you get sticky molasses. Turning it into crystalline sugar took special training. Hooper imported copper boiling pans from China and Chinese workers to run them. Slowly, the many innovations he developed began paying off. Hooper shipped thirty tons of sugar in the 1837-38 season, and he had time to worry that Ladd & Co.'s reputation might be damaged if brewers used Koloa molasses to make rum.

Hooper exhausted himself trying to keep the plantation and sugar mill operating, and in 1839, he was pleased to be succeeded by Charles Burnham. Hooper remained hopeful about the future of sugar at Koloa, but was resolved that it would always be hard work. "It only wants enterprise and capital and perseverance, and it will reach to a point to which no other spot, at these islands, ever can reach," he wrote.

Koloa's land in cane reached 500 acres in the early 1840s, and it was far more than Hooper's second mill could handle. Burnham and Ladd & Co. built a third mill away from Maulili Pond on Waihohonu Stream. Despite the new management and the new equipment, Koloa's sugar remained of poor quality. That changed only after a French sugar processor named Victor Prevost spent a year training Ladd & Co.'s team in the secrets of "tempering, clarifying, boiling and granulating of sugars."

But despite the advances in quality of product, the plantation was in desperate financial condition. Ladd & Co. was deeply in debt to the Hawaiian government, both for rent and loans made by the government to the company. The crown was demanding repayment of its several mortgages on both the crops and the plantation itself. In the plantation's tenth year, all Ladd & Co.'s property at Kōloa was sold in a sheriff's sale, and the government of the Kingdom of Hawai'i acquired a half-interest in the plantation. Burnham left, and the management was turned over to James N. Lindsey.

After a series of complex negotiations and court proceedings, Dr. Robert W. Wood, one of the creditors of the plantation, got title to it in 1848, and it was renamed Koloa Plantation. Wood was a physician and drug store operator. He obtained a fifty-year lease on the sugar lands and the mill. The plantation at the time covered 2,200 acres.

Koloa Plantation apparently was on solid financial footing by 1850, producing $20,000 in sugar that cost $10,000 to grow and process. Wood was looking for someone to run the plantation for him, and in 1851 sold a half-interest for $25,000 to lawyer Samuel Burbank, who agreed that he would work without compensation and would pay the $25,000 out of the company's

Top: Soil for the Waitā Reservoir dam was collected in part from a borrow pit on the slopes of Waihohonu Hill in 1905 and 1906 and hauled to the dam site by train.
Bottom: One of the plantation's two locomotives—the Paulo—is still operable today. Kaua'i's first locomotive, Paulo (shown here in 1936) was purchased in 1888 and later refurbished by Grove Farm Homestead Museum. The Haupu does not survive. Both were Hohenzollern-type locomotives manufactured in Dusseldorf, Germany and shipped to Hawai'i around Cape Horn.

"Wow, Grove Farm bought into history!"

Pat Agustin's father, Timoteo, a 1918 immigrant from the Philippines, was a contract irrigator with Grove Farm. The family lived first at Halehaka Valley and then at Puhi Camp. Three of Timoteo's seven children were Philippines-born and four were born on Kaua'i, including Pat. He was born in 1930.

He attended Lihue Grammar School and Kauai High School, where Coach Akio Kubota taught him sportsmanship.

Pat started with Grove Farm, he recalls precisely, on Sept. 13, 1950, when he was nineteen. His career would span forty-five and a half years. He started as a janitor in the company shop, then as a painter helper and then a full-time journeyman painter.

"If you were interested, Grove Farm would send you to learn other things. I learned welding. I'm part of the gang who built Koloa Mill—in the off-season, they would let people go in the mill and do welding projects," he said.

His brother, Demetrio "Deme" Agustin, was also a painter, but doubled up during Grove Farm's tunnel construction era driving the truck that lifted blast debris and dumped it into rail cars. With his father, himself, two brothers and a brother-in-law, the Agustin family had close to 200 years of service with Grove Farm, Pat said.

"I've seen the changes at Grove Farm. I remember the dusty roads. Houses were all open, welcoming people to come in. Neighbors would call you in the house to talk story. The plantation camp was something.

"We had two company stores and the camp store, Funada Store. The company stores, Amby Fernandez Store and Sun Len Chong Store, they would let you charge to your *bango* (employee number). My number was 817 and later 2817. That was my father's bango, too, 817. At Funada Store, they only took cash.

"We would sit in the park in front of the Grove Farm office and count the cars passing. You never dreamed there would be traffic congestion.

"When Grove Farm bought Koloa, I thought, *Wow, Grove Farm bought into history—the oldest sugar plantation!*

"And I remember when the company went out of sugar. The changes were all coming. Hard to stop it."

Potenciano "Pat" Agustin

profits. Burbank died before he could complete his purchase, but he made several major changes during his roughly ten years there. One of his first jobs was to rebuild the factory water wheel. Burbank used a double mold-board plow to deep-plow the sugar fields, an invention that was adopted by other plantations across the archipelago. He drained the vast Kōloa Marsh using a series of ditches in hopes of creating fertile cane land, but the peat soils did not grow sugar cane well. The first irrigation ditch, or "water lead," at Koloa was installed in 1869 by manager George Dole with George Charman. It was an emergency effort to get water to dying cane during a particularly dry period.

The Great Māhele permitted fee simple ownership of land in the kingdom, and Koloa Plantation began converting its sugar growing leases to fee title and expanding its acreage. Its mill site on Waihohonu Stream remained a lease. In 1871 Wood, who was in poor health, sold off his interest in the plantation. He sold half of his interest in the plantation to Lihue Plantation manager Paul Isenberg, and a quarter each to John N. Wright and Adolf Haneberg. Wright would operate the plantation. Koloa Plantation expanded its farming into Māhā'ulepū Valley in 1878 on a lease, and later began buying up lands from native members of the Mahaulepu Hui. (Māhā'ulepū is the modern spelling, but in the days of the *hui*, diacritical marks were not used.) The number of owners of the Koloa sugar operation expanded as the new owners sold full or partial interests in their own stakes.

Anton Cropp, Koloa manager from 1882 to 1900, reportedly was as aggressive a ditch builder as George Norton Wilcox and was able to irrigate many of Koloa's sugar fields. But the south side of Kaua'i was not water rich, and he got much of that irrigation water from Grove Farm. Cropp also oversaw the switch from oxcarts to rail starting in 1888, and the first locomotive was Paulo, named for Paul Isenberg. That locomotive, more than 125 years old, is still in working condition after extensive refurbishment by Grove Farm Homestead Museum.

Koloa's field mechanization matched Grove Farm's. Twelve-horsepower Fowler steam plows arrived in 1893. But Koloa had a mill to keep modern as well. In 1885 Cropp matched a three-roller mill with a separate two-roller mill, which removed enough cane juice that the remaining bagasse was dry enough to use directly in the mill boilers. In 1897, another three-roller mill was installed, along with a new vacuum pan, boiler and centrifuges.

Water for irrigation continued to be an issue. Koloa Plantation added to its Wilcox Ditch water with six wells drilled at Māhāʻulepū, each with an estimated capacity of a million gallons per day.

The overthrow of the Hawaiian monarchy in 1893, leading to the 1898 annexation by the United States, created a labor uproar. Hawaiian labor contracts were declared null and plantation workers were free to sell their services wherever the offer was best. Koloa Plantation did not have serious problems with lack of labor, but it continued to have water issues. On Cropp's departure, Patrick McLane was named manager. Two of McLane's young supervisors were nephews of Grove Farm's George N. Wilcox: Gaylord P. Wilcox, who would later run Kealia Plantation, and Charles H. Wilcox, who would later manage Koloa Plantation.

McLane expanded sugarcane lands into the dry Paʻa and Weliweli areas. At the annual meeting of 1901, Hans Isenberg, the brother of Paul Isenberg, worried that Koloa Plantation did not have sufficient water resources to irrigate all its cane through the dry season. McLane agreed, saying that efforts to locate artesian water and to tunnel for water had proven fruitless. He began planning aggressive water storage measures in the form of a series of reservoirs. He expanded the Wilcox Ditch so that it would carry more water during rainstorms, which would be used to fill the reservoirs. At that time, Wilcox Ditch drew water from streams along the south side, the Kōloa side, of the Hāʻupu Range. McLane also proposed recycling mill processing water and using it for irrigation as well.

But nothing matched McLane's development of what was then called the Marsh Reservoir—which would eventually be the largest reservoir in the Hawaiian Islands. The Kōloa Marsh that Burbank had drained would be dammed and filled. Hans Isenberg supported the measure, although McLane's plan also had stockholder opposition for various reasons, including cost and complexity. Among the opponents was Anton Cropp who owned a significant share of the company. He argued that it was folly to give up cane land near the mill, but other directors were swayed by the value of the water storage and the fact that the marsh did

Top: Store employees Satsuyo Yamada and Rosita Semana stand by tables of merchandise inside Grove Farm's Koloa Store (exterior, right) in 1949.

KOLOA PLANTATION 39

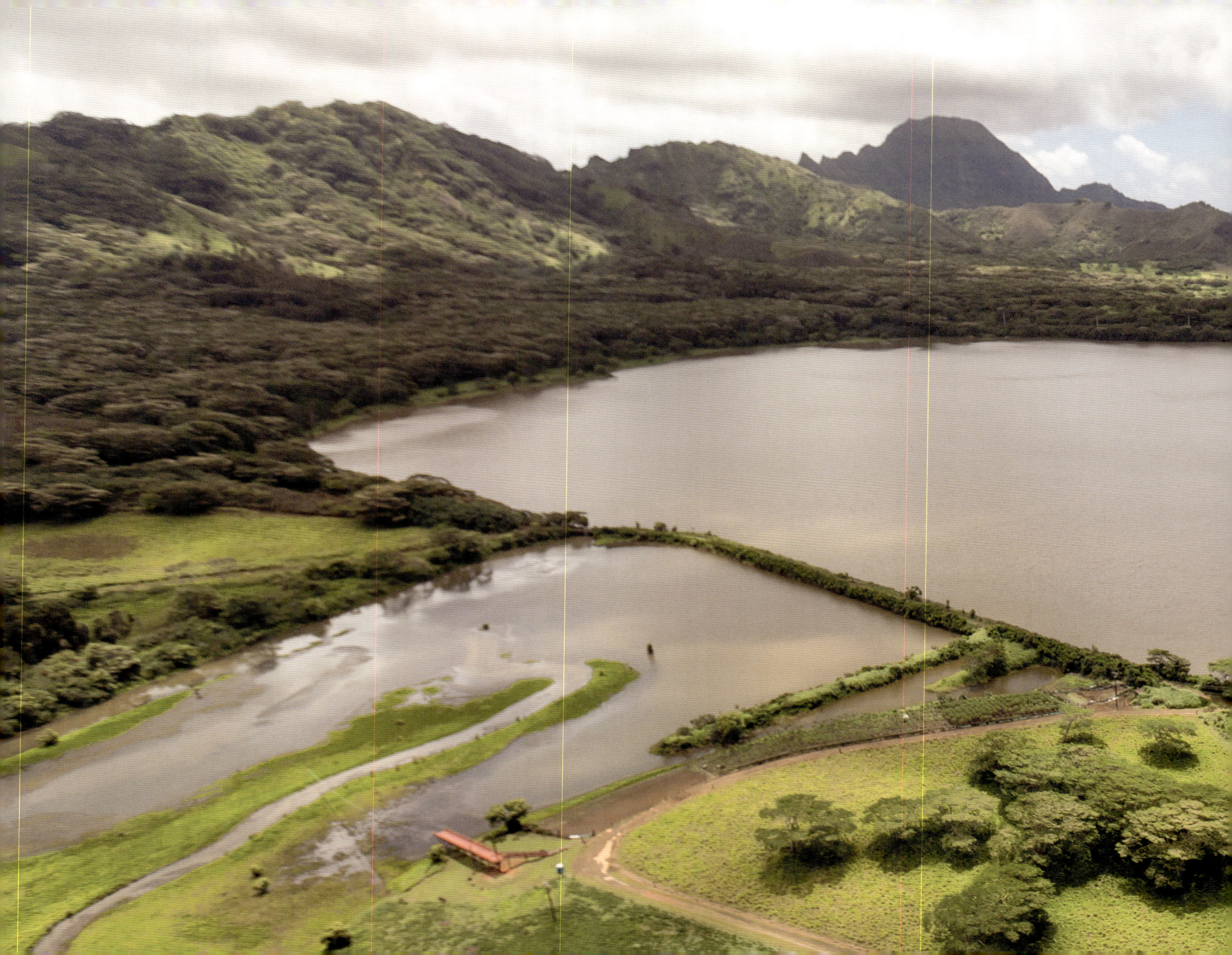

Recognizing that the Kōloa area did not have its own rich water resources, Koloa Plantation developed the Waitā Reservoir into a water storage facility that now covers more acreage than any other reservoir in the state of Hawai'i. Today it is still fed water from Kuʻia Stream on the other side of the Hāʻupu Range.

Early sugar cane crushers were granite cylinders fitted with wooden gears in slots, turned by livestock as stalks of cane were hand-loaded and cane juice was collected on a flat stone beneath them.
Top: *A model at Grove Farm Homestead Museum.*
Above Left: *An actual crusher on display at the 1935 Koloa Centennial Celebration.*
Above Right: *Railroad cane cars are lined up in 1930, leading toward the Koloa Mill. Note mill camp houses to the left of the factory, and numerous* panini *(prickly pear cactus) in the field to the right.*
Right: *Koloa Mill ground sugar cane for Koloa Plantation, Grove Farm and McBryde Sugar Company, before being taken out of service in the late 1990s. Although the mill is structurally unsafe and scheduled for demolition, the site remains an industrial-zoned area that will continue to serve the needs of the Kōloa area.*

42   GROVE FARM: LEGACY OF THE LAND

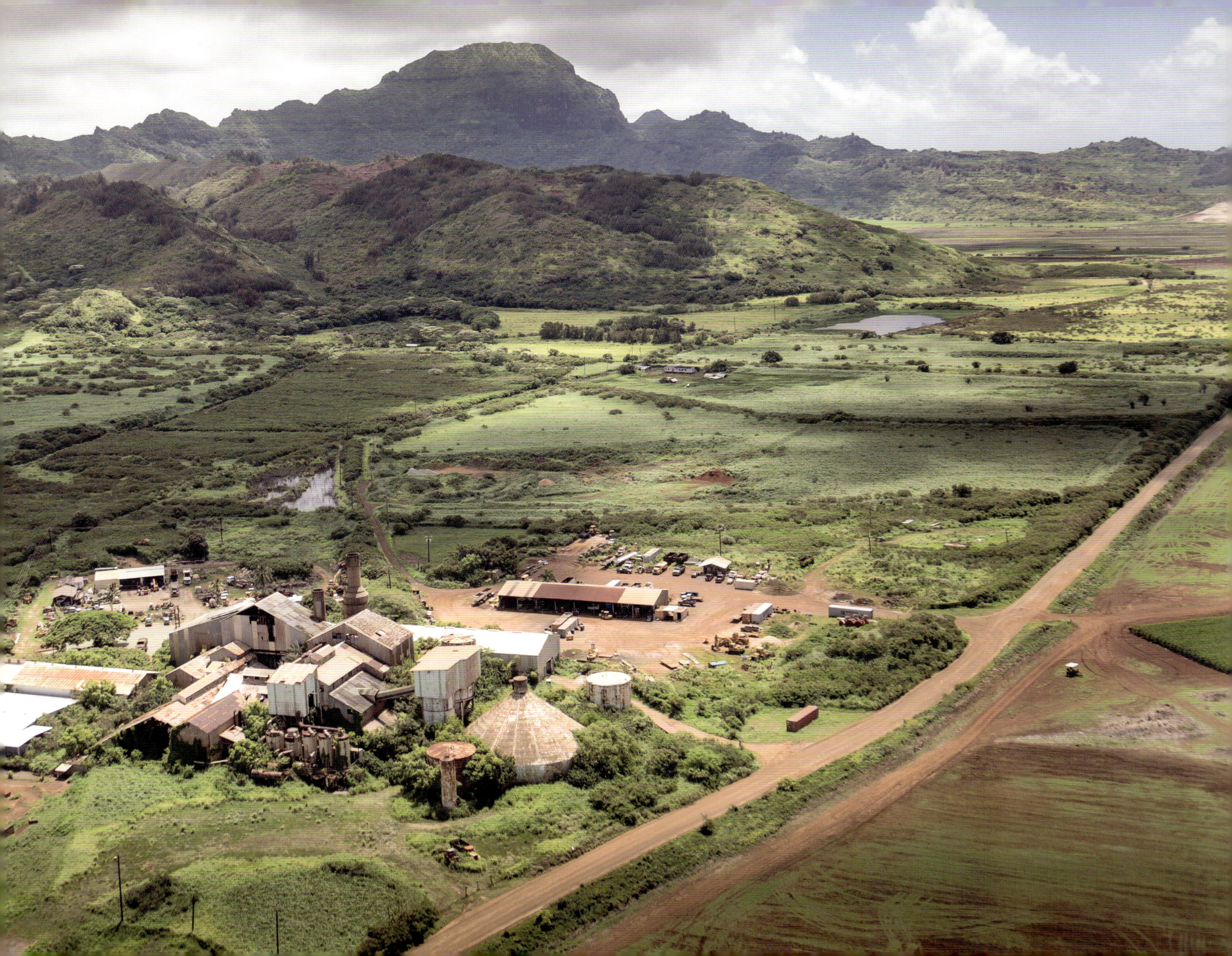

not grow cane well anyway.

There were plenty of issues. The marsh was deep and muddy and a watertight dam would need to find a solid bottom. Caves and lava tubes could drain away water. But the benefit was a reservoir that could potentially store a billion gallons of water for the plantation, McLane told his directors. In January 1905, they authorized him to start small, on a 300 million-gallon reservoir that could be increased in capacity later. It was done by April, and filled to capacity in late fall.

And despite the concerns of detractors, it held water. In January 1906, the directors authorized the dam be built higher, to McLane's full proposed capacity. But in February 1906, in a coup led by Cropp, McLane was dismissed. He moved on to successfully run a sugar plantation in Puerto Rico. The expanded dam was his signature project, and it proceeded. The Marsh Reservoir expansion was completed in May 1906. By January 1907 it exceeded McLane's own estimates. It held 1.5 billion gallons. It was so successful that new manager Ludwig Weinzheimer was authorized in June 1908 to add another five feet to the dam height, increasing its capacity to 2.5 billion gallons. The next year, he accepted a job running Pioneer Mill on Maui, and Charles H. Wilcox was appointed manager of Koloa Plantation.

For all its sophistication, the sugar-processing factory on Waihohonu Stream was problematic. It was on leased land, and the equipment and design were aging. The company decided in 1912 to build a new factory on fee simple land in Pa‘a. Honolulu Iron Works would build the machinery. It was sited so that it could use water from the Marsh Reservoir, and that waste mill water could go into the Kalaiokehoni Reservoir for use in irrigation. The mill was completed in 1913, an advanced design with twelve rollers and an automatic feed system that took bagasse directly from the grinding mills to the boilers.

Charles Wilcox left Koloa to join his uncle, George, at Grove Farm in 1913, and Koloa was turned over to Ernest Cropp, a nephew of Anton Cropp. Water was still an issue. One summer, the Marsh Reservoir had run dry. Koloa arranged with Lihue Plantation to acquire some of its surplus water, which would pass over Grove Farm land to

Completed in 1915, the irrigation ditch was a massive undertaking, its longest tunnel 5,845 feet in length.

Top: In 1951, plantations were switching from shipping sugar in bags to sending it off in bulk containers. Here, Alex Sagun stiches closed Koloa Mill's last bag of sugar, as Chisei Oyasato records the operation and Magno Albero looks on.
Left: In the Koloa Mill boiling house in 1956, Kakuichi Fukumoto works as a pan man on the pan floor.
Opposite: As Koloa Plantation struggled with water issues, one of its solutions was a series of wells in the Māhā‘ulepū area. In the days before roads and trucks were common on the plantation, residential hamlets were established near work sites. The Mahaulepu Pump Camp is shown here in 1930.

be delivered by ditch and aqueduct from Wai‘ahi-Kū‘ia to the Wilcox Ditch and thus into the Marsh Reservoir. The new ditch passed through what was then called Kōloa Gap and is now commonly called Knudsen Gap. Most of the length of its 3.3 miles was underground. The system had 14,685 feet in tunnel, 2,320 feet in ditch and 467 feet crossing valleys in flumes. It was a massive undertaking; the longest tunnel 5,845 feet in length. It was completed in 1915. In 1919, a spur was added, diverting water from Hāli‘i Stream into the ditch.

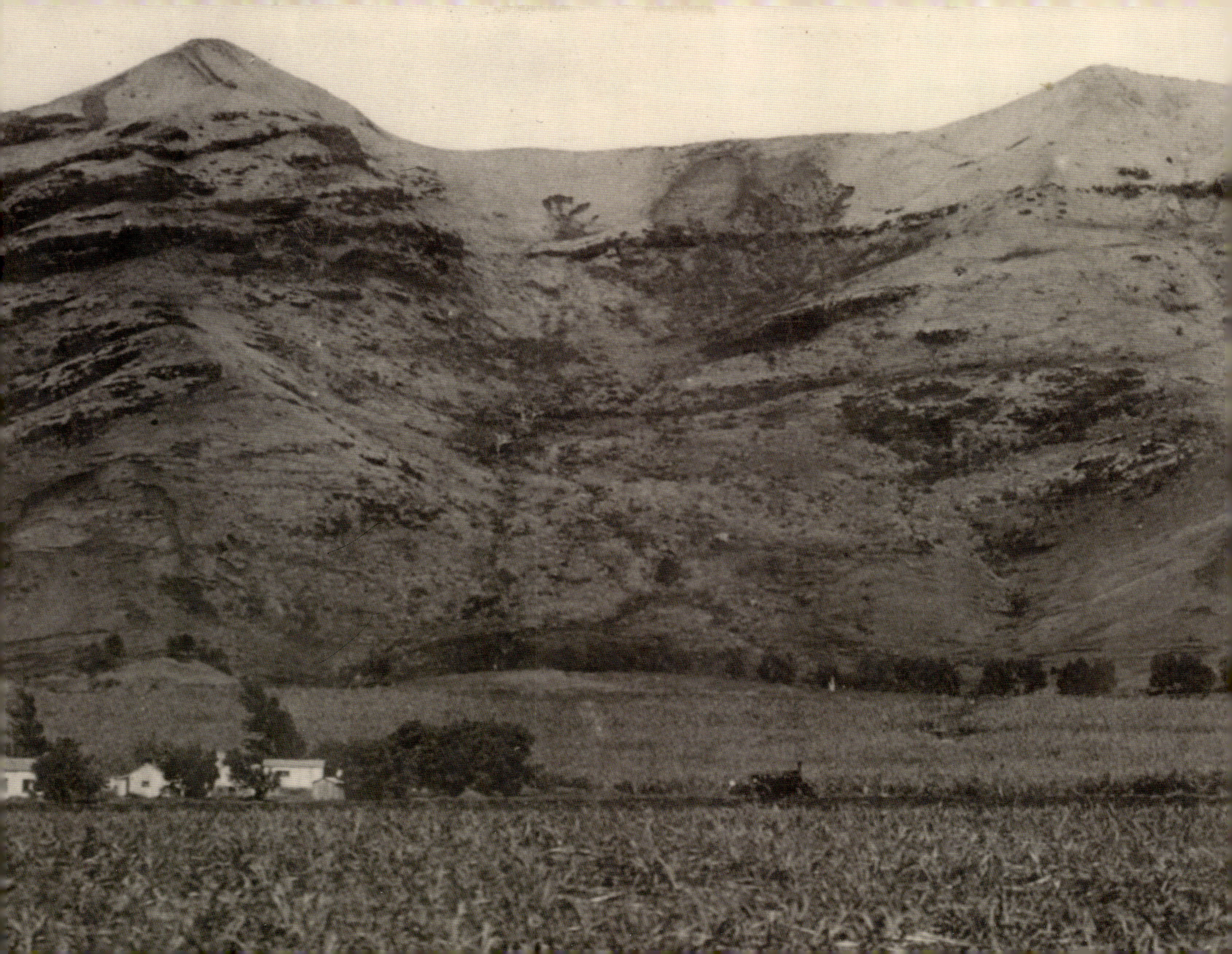

1835 *1935*

The Koloa Sugar Company

requests the pleasure of your presence at the

100th Anniversary Celebration

of the founding of

Ladd and Company

on Saturday, the twenty-seventh of July, 1935

at the Office grounds

Koloa, Kauai.

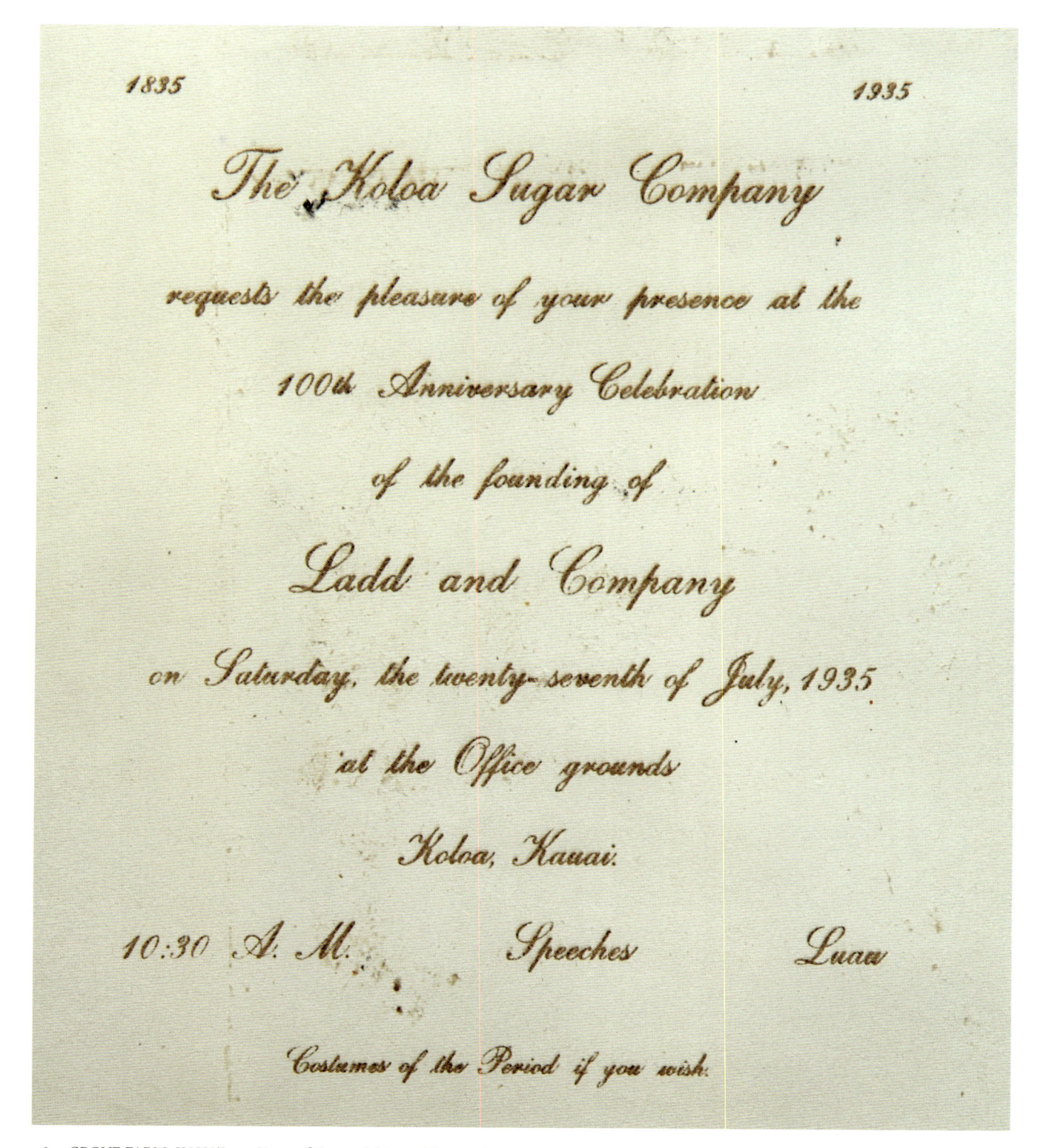

10:30 A. M.   Speeches   Luau

Costumes of the Period if you wish.

KOLOA FIRM'S ANNIVERSARY

Beginning of Sugar Industry 100 Years Ago Depicted By Kauai Plantation

(Pictures on Page 3)
(Special Star-Bulletin Correspondence)

KOLOA, Kauai, July 29. — The grounds of Koloa Sugar Co.'s office, the site of the initiation of sugar growing on a commercial scale in Hawaii was Saturday the scene of the centennial celebration of that event.

These grounds, where a prosperous plantation celebrated with a luau for 4,000 people, were the locale of that venture which was begun by three young Yankees — William Hooper, William Ladd and Peter Allan Brinsmade. It was here that the perseverance, ingenuity and determination of William Hooper made the growing and milling of sugar an actuality, and it was here that these three men lost their property under the auctioneer's hammer December 9, 1844.

A short program was given to commemorate the efforts of the founders of Ladd & Co. Hector Moir, manager, and H. A. Walker, president of the Koloa Sugar Co., both declared that although Hooper, Ladd and Brinsmade apparently were failures, their efforts had laid the foundations for the sugar industry which is today the backbone of Hawaii.

Mrs. Margaret Thurston Hatch, a descendant of Hooper and Miss Mabel C. Ladd of Honolulu, descendant

Above: *A 1935 article in* The Honolulu Star-Bulletin *covers the celebration of the first century of Koloa Plantation's history. Although there were sugar plantations before Koloa, the company is widely known as the oldest, and it developed several unique features of modern plantations.*
Opposite: *It's formal attire for the celebration of Koloa Sugar Company's centennial (left), as workers open a massive* imu.

Koloa Plantation built a 120-kilowatt hydroelectric plant using water from the Waiʻahi-Kuʻia aqueduct in 1918, to help power the mill and various pumps.

On Cropp's 1922 retirement, Caleb E.S. Burns would be named manager, followed almost immediately by John T. Moir. They lined the Mill Ditch in concrete, which fed from the Marsh Reservoir to the new mill. Water loss had been a significant problem and the concrete lining conserved the water.

In 1925 and 1926, the plantation installed a massive pumping system that would allow Marsh Reservoir water to be delivered to the higher-elevation Wilcox Ditch so that it could be used to irrigate sugar cane at Kaluahonu and Puhi, which were short of irrigation water. It was a wet year in 1926, and with irrigation needs down, the Waiʻahi-Kūʻia aqueduct was shut down for an expansion project, increasing its capacity from sixty-five to ninety million gallons daily.

There were occasions during heavy rain that the Marsh Reservoir would overflow, creating the risk of erosion of its dam. The top of the dam was raised another three feet in 1931, and at the same time, the interior of the dam was lined with rock to prevent wave erosion. The reservoir, covering several hundred acres, was so massive that waves developed during windy periods that could wear away the interior dam face. Eventually, the rising water flooded the dam between two reservoirs, Hauiki Reservoir and the Marsh Reservoir, creating a body of water that would be known as the Kōloa Reservoir and later the Waitā Reservoir.

Despite its massive capacity, the reservoir was dry in 1933. One problem was that when the weather was dry, it was dry across the island, and there was little surplus water from Lihue Plantation and Grove Farm lands that could be sent to Koloa. John T. Moir left Koloa in 1933, replaced by his brother, Hector Moir. An agricultural expert, Hector Moir worked hard on improving field operations and turned Koloa Plantation into one of the territory's lowest-cost producers of sugar. But that was not enough.

KOLOA PLANTATION

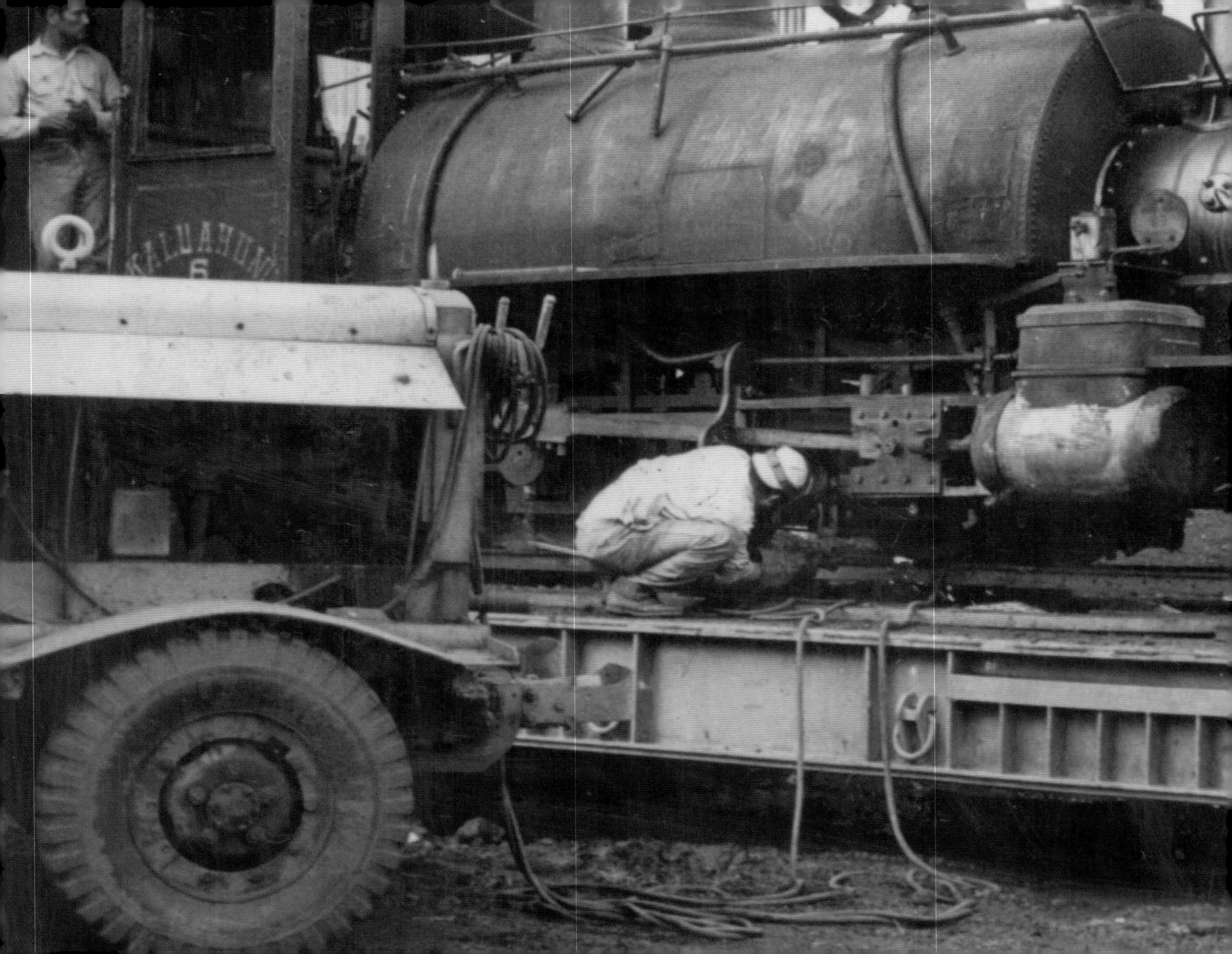

Opposite: *In 1952, Danny Moke watches from the cab and Toshihiro Otani welds, stabilizing wedges beneath the Kaluahonu, Koloa Mill's last steam locomotive, in preparation for shipment out of Koloa. The engine was dismantled and no longer exists, but several of its sister locomotives have been restored to operational use at Grove Farm Homestead Museum.*

Above: *Most of the equipment in the old mill in Kōloa Town was moved to Koloa Sugar Company's new mill, completed in 1913 on fee simple land in Pa'a.*

Left: *Hawaiian sugar mills went through smokestacks with some regularity. A new mill stack is erected at Koloa Mill in 1954, as the old one stands in the background. The plantation brought most or all of its cranes into use during these operations.*

KOLOA PLANTATION

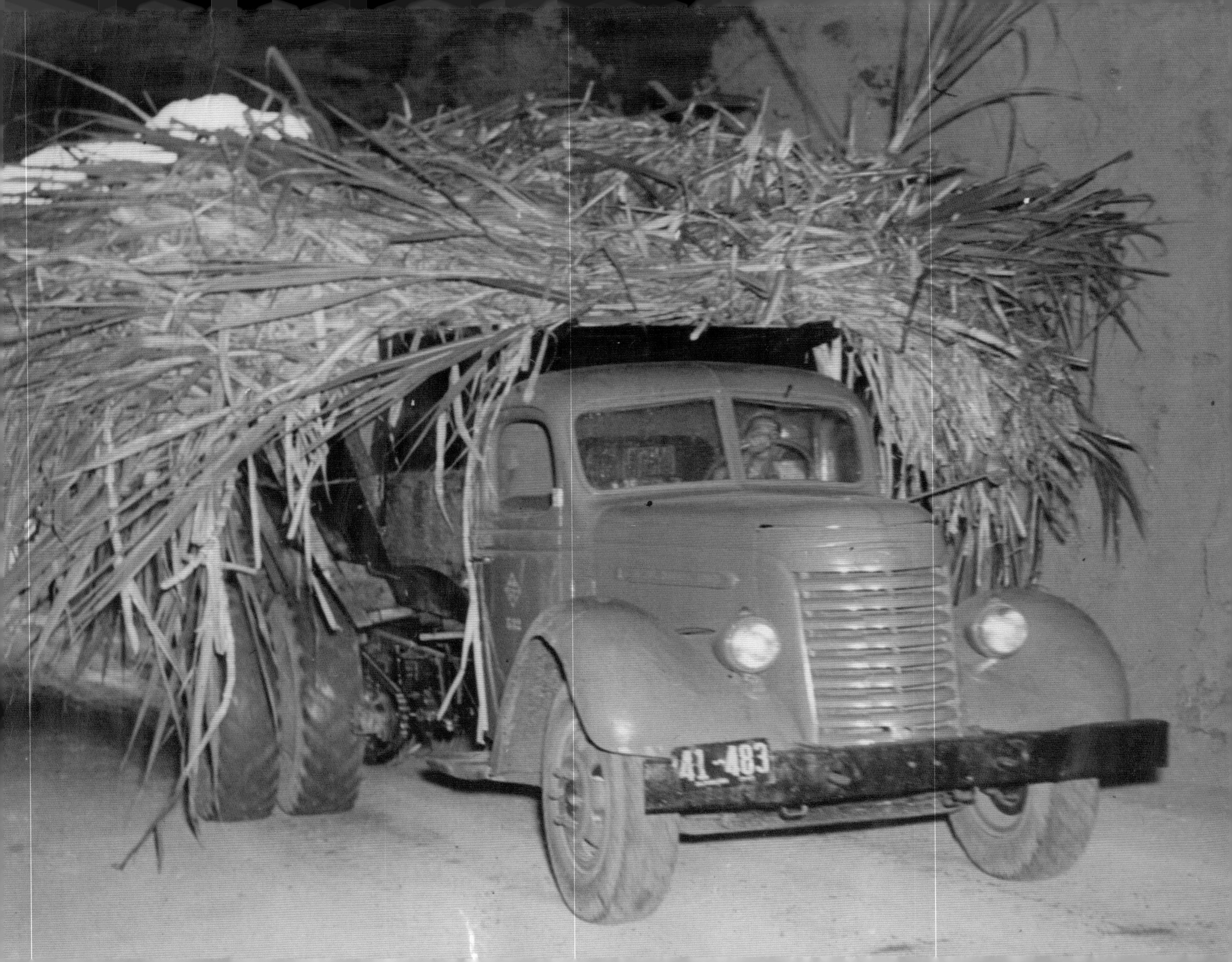
41-483

During the next decade, the company's inherent problems began catching up with it. It was small and suffered from all the problems of a small sugar plantation unable to benefit from economies of scale. It was hit by the labor shortages caused by World War II, its continued water issues and the increased labor costs associated with unionization. By the late 1940s, the firm had roughly $1 million in debt and there was significant deferred maintenance in the factory. The Koloa Plantation owners—at this time, primarily Amfac—were seeking ways to solve their problem.

The obvious partnerships involved McBryde Sugar to the west and Grove Farm to the east. Both expressed interest. Grove Farm stockholders in December 1947 approved a proposal to buy Koloa Plantation and the deal was done.

The plantations were separated by the Hā'upu Range, but Grove Farm's operations manager Bill Moragne oversaw the construction of the tunnel that effectively combined the plantations, and provided Grove Farm sugar cane with a shorter route to the Koloa Mill, entirely on land owned by the company. The tunnel was twenty feet tall and twenty feet wide, capable of hauling a single heavily loaded cane truck. It was only one lane wide, but straight, so you could see as you entered whether there was another vehicle in the tunnel.

Opposite: *The first truckload of sugar cane is driven through the new Wilcox Tunnel in 1950. Grove Farm built the tunnel through the Hā'upu Range to transport cane to the Koloa Mill, after it bought Koloa Sugar Company.*

"Grove Farm treated me real well."

Perfecto Labrador, 84, was a sickly boy, born in 1930 to the Philippines-born stablemaster at Koloa Plantation, Andres Labrador. They lived in a house near the stables, where his father could get up at 1 a.m. to help feed and ready the horses and other livestock for work on the plantation. His dad learned about horses, he said, from a Hawaiian friend named Martin.

Perfecto suffered from a weak heart as a boy. "Doctors told my parents, 'If he die, die.' I never did go high school. I would have to sleep after lunch and before dinner," he said. As he became an adult, his heart strengthened. "I came out the healthiest one. All my brothers passed away."

His language is scattered with Hawaiian words that are no longer common. He recalls that field workers would bring their own *kālai* or hoe, to *huki lepo* or pull dirt—either to clear weeds or build furrows or cover seed cane. Many young boys did such work during weekends and summers. Perfecto did, too. He recalls his weak heart forced him to take breaks, and the other boys covered for him.

When planting cane, he said, after the furrows had been built, one worker would walk along dropping cut stalks of cane. The next would line up the stalks butt-to-butt. The third worker would walk along and huki lepo, covering the cane stalks with dirt, and finally older workers would irrigate—turning water into the furrows to water the new cane.

Then there was harvesting. "One guy cut the cane, that's all he did, cut, cut, cut. One guy piled it up. And one guy, the hāpai kō (carry cane), he would put a stick under the pile and grab it and carry the pile to the cart. That was the hardest job," he said.

Perfecto worked for a time as a truck driver for the construction firm HC&D in Honolulu. He married a Kaumakani girl and came to Grove Farm in 1950, first as a field hand and then in the shop. He went to school to study diesel mechanics, specializing in Detroit and Caterpillar equipment. He also leased space from Grove Farm to run his own diesel repair shop.

"I never refuse hard work. My father told me, the boss was God. Our family, all hard workers." When he started work for Grove Farm, Perfecto lived at Mill Camp in Kōloa, Puhi Camp and then Puhi subdivision. Today, he lives in a lot developed by Grove Farm at Ulu Ko.

"Dave Pratt gave us first preference on the lot. Grove Farm treated me real well."

Perfecto Labrador

Fully loaded cane carts, hauled by oxen, head for the factory in about 1888. G.N. Wilcox is on horseback at center, while Lihue Plantation's Paul R. Isenberg is the second horseman from left. The managers regularly inspected their field operations on horseback.

Chapter 3
Lihue Plantation

"The new Grove Farm-Lihue Plantation contract had just been signed... I said to Mr. (George N.) Wilcox that it was a very good contract for Grove Farm, and he said, 'Yes, but it's more than that. It's a very good contract for Lihue Plantation. That's the way every contract should be. It should be completely fair to both sides or it won't hold up.'"
—William P. Alexander

"G.N. (Wilcox) told me once in great confidence that when Paul Isenberg left to go back to Germany, he offered G.N. his controlling interest in Lihue Plantation. G.N. thought it was a bigger obligation than he could take over, consequently he did not take up the offer."
—Gaylord P. Wilcox

Hawai'i's sugar plantations were connected to each other in ways unlike most other industries. They shared resources like water, shared transportation systems like railway systems, sometimes shared factories and often shared ownership.

And Lihue Plantation was among the most interconnected of them all.

As an example, Paul Isenberg was an early manager of Lihue Plantation, but also owned half of Koloa Plantation. Paul Isenberg and Grove Farm's George Norton Wilcox founded Kekaha Sugar Company.

Grove Farm milled its cane initially at Lihue Plantation's Lihue Mill. Much of the irrigation water for Koloa Plantation flowed from water sources controlled and developed by Lihue Plantation and Grove Farm.

Many of the Kaua'i sugar plantations connected their plantation railways, largely to allow sugar to be transported all the way to the harbor—even by plantations without their own harbors. But the connected railway system also allowed unwieldy plantation equipment to travel from the harbor to the plantations. And the railways allowed other plantations to ship gear for repair to neighboring factories with specialized machining capacity, as Lihue Plantation's mill metal shop possessed.

The connection of all the railways from Līhu'e to Waimea was a requirement of federal support for the development of Nāwiliwili Harbor.

The various kinds of interconnectedness of early in sugar's Hawaiian history, there was a lot of contact and cross-pollination.

Sugar had been active in the Islands for nearly fifty years when Lihue Plantation was launched in 1849. Work started on Lihue Plantation, a partnership in which Henry A. Peirce owned half the plantation, and Judge William L. Lee and Charles Reed Bishop shared equally in the other half. The initial capitalization was $16,000.

Peirce had played a role in starting the firm that would become C. Brewer & Co. Bishop started Bishop Bank (now First Hawaiian Bank) and married Princess Bernice Pauahi Bishop. Lee, an attorney and later chief justice of the Kingdom's Supreme Court, had a small farm at Kahuku on O'ahu. (Interestingly, Hermann Widemann, from whom George N. Wilcox would buy Grove Farm, was also a member of the Hawaiian Supreme Court.)

The first lands for the Lihue plantation were purchased from the Princess Victoria Kamāmalu, and lay on the broad plateau between the Nāwiliwili and Hanamā'ulu Streams. The plantation and mill were started by manager James H.B. Marshall, an American merchant who had previously done work with Ladd & Co. at Kōloa. On leaving Lihue Plantation, Marshall moved south across Nāwiliwili Valley and joined Judge Hermann A. Widemann in his cane-growing operation—the plantation that a decade later would be George N. Wilcox's Grove Farm. Marshall would still later buy a small ownership interest in Lihue Plantation.

Back at Lihue, the management of the plantation

Sugar had been active in the islands for nearly fifty years when Lihue Plantation was launched in 1849.

the plantations did not necessarily start out that way. In many cases it developed over time. Many of the plantations were started independently by entrepreneurs of the mid 1800s. But even from

Right: In 1899, Lihue Plantation manager Paul Isenberg built a mountain house on the rim of Kilohana Crater, with a view across Lihue Plantation's fields. The two-story home, called Kukaua, here in about 1905, boasted stables, separate servants' quarters and a fruit orchard.

54 GROVE FARM, KAUA'I: 150 Years of Stewardship and Innovation

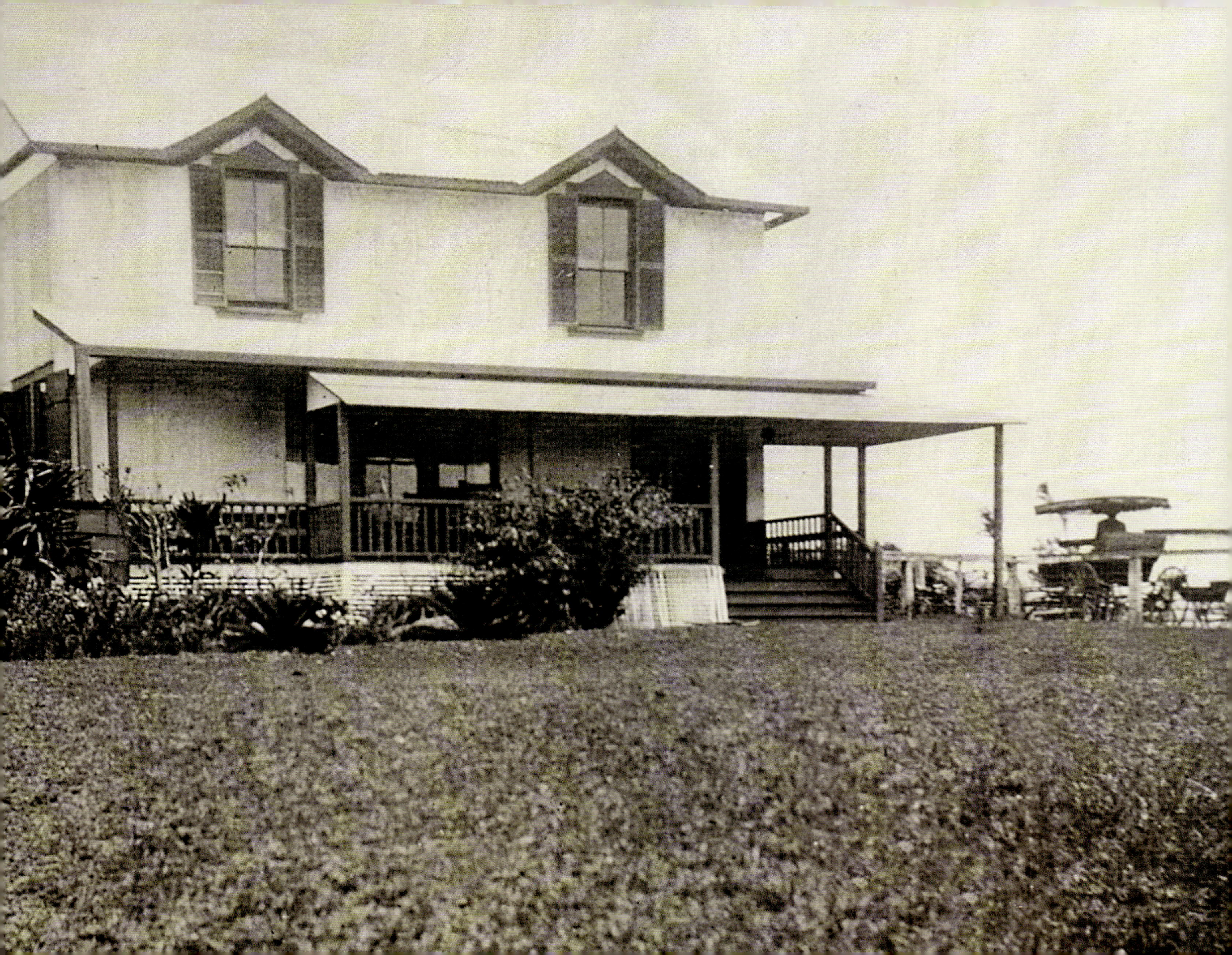

Iliahi Estate, built by former Lihue Plantation manager Caleb Burns, is used today for special events and celebrations. The home, located halfway up the slope of Kilohana Crater, has a commanding view over the Līhu'e plain.

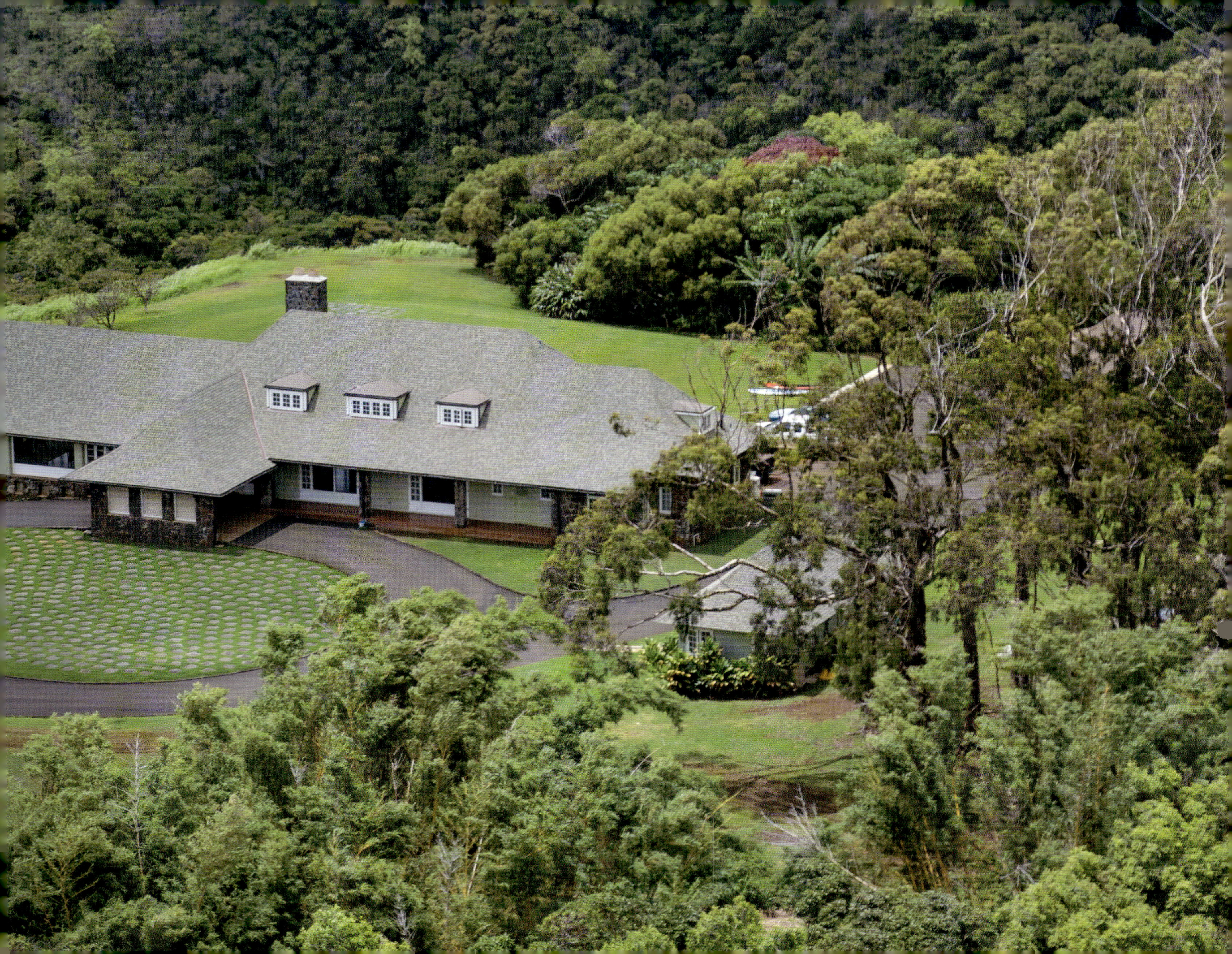

Lihue, Kauai, Hawaii

Opposite: *View of Nāwiliwili taken from Charles Rice's home in 1910, looking toward Hoary Head, also known as Hā'upu Mountain.*
Top: *In July 1933, a full house shows up at Wilcox Gym for the changing of the guard at Koloa Sugar Company. John T. "Jack" Moir and his family were moving from Koloa to Pioneer Mill on Maui, while his brother, Hector Moir, and family were taking over at Koloa. The various Moirs are lei-bedecked in the front row: from left, John T. Moir III, John T. Moir, Mildred Mae Moir, Gertrude Moir, Alexandra Knudsen Moir and Alexandra's husband, Hector Moir.*
Above: *The mill room inside Koloa Mill in 1950 shows off the complex machinery of a modern sugar mill, including the massive open gears and flywheel.*

"That old truck is going to keep you working."

David Nobriga, 87, was raised on Kipu Plantation—his father worked on the former sugar plantation neighboring Grove Farm, which is now a cattle ranch. His grandfather had come from Portugal to work at Lihue Plantation and lived in Hanamā'ulu. Nobriga attended Huleia School, which no longer exists, and then Kauai High School.

He had worked, as did many other kids, summers and weekends in agricultural jobs—like planting corn to feed cattle and hogs. But he really wanted to be a mechanic.

"I talked to Mr. (Bill) Moragne, who was the assistant manager then. I could fix a bicycle but I didn't know much else. He started me as a shop hand in the blacksmith shop and then the machine shop, then welding, and finally in 1946 I got into the automotive shop under Lloyd Nelson."

Grove Farm continued to use steam trains until 1955, but Nobriga did not work on them. He said John Silva was the mechanic for the locomotives.

The company bought a lot of war surplus equipment in the late 1940s, and Nobriga specialized in both automotive and tractor mechanics. He worked on air brakes and the surplus Jeeps that supervisors drove. They worked on the trucks that hauled rock from the quarry—also equipment that had been bought used.

Nobriga remembers complaining about the age of the equipment Grove Farm operated. "I asked Nelson when this company was going to buy new equipment. He said, 'That old truck is going to keep you working.'"

When Grove Farm bought Koloa Plantation, the Puhi-based mechanics did repairs and rebuilding of equipment for both plantations. Sometimes they went into the field to repair gear, like the compressors being used in tunnel building.

Sometimes they would work on one compressor while another one was operating right alongside. "Holy cats, they were loud," Nobriga said.

When Grove Farm leased out its sugar fields, Nobriga went to McBryde for three years, but then came back in 1978 to Grove Farm again to work in its machine shop. He stayed until his 1993 retirement.

David Nobriga

LIHUE PLANTATION 59

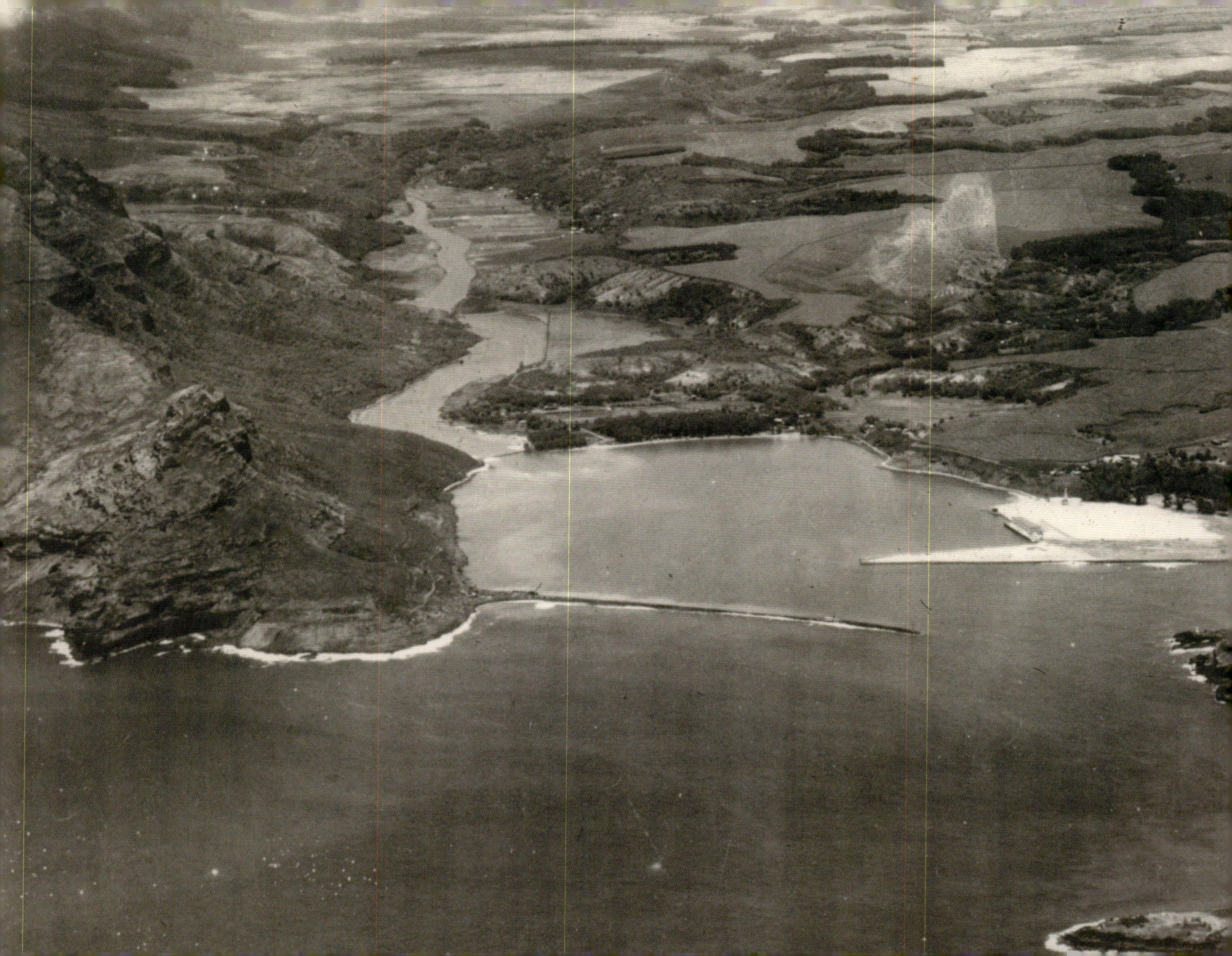

was turned over to agriculturalist William Harrison Rice. The great innovation of Rice, who suffered from tuberculosis, was the construction of irrigation systems to carry the cane through dry summers. Rice built some of the first irrigation ditches. His Rice Ditch in 1856 was said to be the first sugar plantation irrigation ditch in the Islands. It was, however, certainly not the first agricultural ditch in the Islands, as Hawaiians centuries earlier had mastered diverting water using ditches to irrigate taro fields.

Did it work? Amazingly well, if you believe the media of the time. The Hawaiian newspaper *The Polynesian* on September 19, 1857, in a front-page story, wrote about the project that it took eleven miles of ditch to convey water a twisting route from the stream to the fields—a distance of only a mile and a quarter as the crow flies.

"Almost as far as the eye can reach, the difference in color and conditions of the fields of cane subjected to irrigation and that beyond is perceptible," the paper wrote. "The system of irrigation introduced with vast labor and great expense is the cause of this effect."

George Norton Wilcox understood this immediately. He built on W.H. Rice's irrigation innovations, and as an engineer, he expanded many of them. Paul Isenberg began contracting with Wilcox to engineer some of Lihue Plantation's irrigation systems at the same time Wilcox was building Grove Farm's own irrigation system.

Lihue Plantation's mill started out as one of the most advanced in the Kingdom and innovations over time would keep it in the technological forefront. The first mill was powered by water from Nāwiliwili Stream using ironclad granite rollers. Rice brought additional water from the Hanamāʻulu Stream to increase the capacity of the mill, but it became clear that the power demands outpaced available water supplies.

The big water wheels were replaced in short order by steam. The first steam engine was installed in 1853, just two years after the mill was opened, and another was added in 1859. Soon, steam was also used to boil sugar. It had significant benefits over open fires—the heat could be turned off with a valve and the smoke was less likely to impact a flavor of the end product.

George Wilcox signed a milling agreement with Paul Isenberg to grind Grove Farm's cane at Lihue Mill, and his first crop was ground and sold in mid-1866. He made nearly a $1,000 profit, but was unhappy at the cost of milling—he received just half the value of the sugar and molasses his cane produced.

Over the years, Wilcox's percentage of the total return improved, but Grove Farm's owner fretted over the lack of control over his plantation's sugar. The frustration built, and when Wilcox felt he was not getting a fair deal, he quietly took a ship for Scotland and in 1876 bought an entire mill and ordered it shipped to Hawaiʻi.

Lihue Plantation's Isenberg quickly launched negotiations with Wilcox. He offered Grove Farm better terms on the grinding of its cane. Lihue Plantation bought Wilcox's mill and installed it at Hanamāʻulu, where the company was expanding its cane farming. Wilcox arranged for his brother Albert, who had been farming in Hanalei, to become the new manager. Lihue's Hanamāʻulu mill was closed in 1920 and parts of it were incorporated into Lihue Mill.

Lihue Plantation would continue to expand when it acquired Makee Sugar in Kealia. Lihue had acquired stock in Makee as early as 1910, but bought the company outright in 1933. Makee's manager Caleb E.S. Burns became Lihue Plantation's manager. He built himself a manager's home halfway up the slopes of Kilohana Crater, overlooking Līhuʻe. Burns had been in the Hawaiian sugar industry since arriving in the Islands from Maine in 1909. He had been manager of Koloa Plantation in 1922.

Left: *Nāwiliwili Bay viewed from the east ca. 1931. George Norton Wilcox pledged his personal wealth to ensure that the commercial harbor was built. The breakwater and jetty are complete, but the commercial area that today includes the small boat harbor has not yet been built.*

While most of the old Makee sugar lands were sold off separately after the closing of Lihue Plantation in 2000, the palatial Burns home was part of the 18,000 acres of Lihue Plantation property acquired by Steve Case in 2001.

Through much of its history, Lihue Plantation grew its own cane, but its mill ground came from Lihue and two other plantations: the Rice family's Kipu Plantation and Grove Farm. Lihue started or acquired plantations to its north—notably Hanamāʻulu and Makee—but maintained processing contracts with its neighbors to the south. That changed during the 1940s, when both Kipu and Grove Farm would end their grinding agreements with Lihue Plantation.

> **What Hawaiian plantations had going for them is that they were rich in Hawaiian land.**

During World War II, Kipu gave up its sugar cane operation and changed its name to Kipu Ranch, switching from farming to ranching. The ranch continues to operate today. In 1948, Grove Farm gave up its contract with Lihue Plantation when it bought Koloa Plantation and began grinding its cane at the Koloa Mill.

But despite the loss of those two plantations, Lihue remained the most productive mill on the island, processing close to fifty percent more cane through the 1960s than its nearest rival, which was Koloa Mill.

The next big change in Lihue's operations came in 1974 when Grove Farm went out of the sugar business and the Lihue Mill regained the production from the roughly 2,800 acres of cane it had lost when Grove Farm acquired Koloa Plantation in 1948.

The mill couldn't handle all the expanded Lihue fields plus the Grove Farm fields. However, the Grove Farm acreage was right next door while some of Lihue's most distant fields required trucking cane many miles, sometimes through urban areas. By adding the Grove Farm acreage, Lihue Plantation was able to abandon some of its farthest-away fields on the east side of Kauaʻi while still keeping the mill operating at capacity.

In retrospect, it was a good move since the oil crisis of the late 70s would cause trucking fuel to skyrocket in price. Still, Lihue Plantation, as big and efficient as it was, grew cane on a windward shore and it never produced near the yields of sunny leeward plantations.

Sugar plantation veterans will say it costs the same to grow a field that yields seven or eight tons of sugar per acre as it does one that yields twelve or fourteen tons. It's just that the latter pays nearly twice as much. One by one Hawaiian windward plantations went out of business, and even leeward plantations suffered from stagnant sugar prices while the cost of operations rose with time.

But what Hawaiian plantations had going for them was that they were rich in Hawaiian land. Lihue Plantation's parent company, Amfac, fought off a series of takeover attempts in the 1970s and 1980s by investors particularly interested in the underlying real estate value.

Amfac's ownership came into play in 1988 when a group of its own managers made an $800 million offer for the company. Other offers soon rushed in and it all came to a head when one of the richest players in the national land development business stepped up.

Chicago real estate firm, JMB Realty, with some $20 billion in real estate under management, was often described as the biggest real estate syndicator in the United States. Its bid to Amfac of $920 million was fifteen percent higher than the Amfac management offer to take the company private, and JMB's bid was accepted.

The deal gave the Chicago firm 55,000 acres of sugar and coffee land on four islands, and included three golf courses. It also gave it Lihue Plantation. The resulting firm Amfac/JMB made significant efforts to save the troubled Lihue Plantation, including involving its employees in the discussion of saving the sugar company. But in 2000, the plantation closed its doors and went on the market.

Steve Case bought 800 acres of non-sugar land around Līhuʻe from Amfac in 2000 and then in 2001, purchased most of the cane land, some 17,800 acres. He did not buy the Lihue Mill, which was sold separately. In 2002, Amfac/JMB declared bankruptcy.

Case held his Lihue Plantation holdings in the name of Lihue Land Co. But those properties would be managed as a unified property with his Grove Farm acreage. The Lihue and Grove Farm lands, so long intertwined in various ways, lie adjacent to each other, sharing a boundary several miles long from the Līhuʻe-Puhi area east to the ridge between Mount Kawaikini and Mount Kāhili. Kilohana Crater, *mauka* of Līhuʻe, is split by the property line between Case's Grove Farm and Lihue Land Co. holdings.

Opposite Top: *Before Nāwiliwili Harbor was built, much of the sugar processed from the Kipu Plantation, Grove Farm and Lihue Plantation fields was shipped out of the small Ahukini Harbor. That harbor's breakwater is shown during its construction from 1921 to 1924. It was designed and built by civil engineer J.H. Moragne for Ahukini Terminal and Railway Company, which was affiliated with Lihue Plantation.*
Opposite Bottom: *A railway was built out onto the breakwater to carry stones for its extension. A locomotive steams at right, and cars loaded with boulders are visible at left center.*

LIHUE PLANTATION 63

Puhi Camp in 1936: New employee housing was built with interior and exterior walls of canec, a panel material made of pressed sugar cane fiber. Introduced to repel termites, the canec houses were soon replaced with concrete homes built with hollow tile.

Chapter 4
Growing Up Grove Farm

"We lived at Aakukui Camp and Kaipu Camp and then Puhi Camp. After that I got married and we bought a house." —Michiye Funaku

"(Mr. Akau) would come with a weird-looking wagon, selling all the Chinese delicacies. 'Manju, manapua, pepeiao!' he would yell." —Bernadette Sakoda

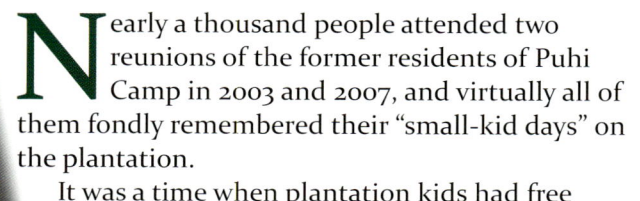

Nearly a thousand people attended two reunions of the former residents of Puhi Camp in 2003 and 2007, and virtually all of them fondly remembered their "small-kid days" on the plantation.

It was a time when plantation kids had free range of the plantation, picking fruits in the valleys, swimming in the reservoirs, hiking through the cane fields and open country, getting sweets at the three camp stores.

And it was a time when people looked out for each other. Parents let children wander the countryside all day long, secure that any and all adults would keep an eye on them. The kids had their own hierarchy, too, and took care of each other.

"You had the young single guys about twenty years old. They had a club, the Pals Club—it didn't mean anything special. They were just pals. Pat Agustin and Chick Cacabelos were two of them. They would take care of us, the younger kids aged eight to ten years old," said Robert H. "Bobby" Agena, now seventy.

Grove Farm had several housing areas in the early years, generally located near where the employees were assigned to work. There were camps at Halfway Bridge, Aakukui, Halehaka Valley, Malumalu, the Grove Farm old headquarters and later Puhi Camp alongside the new headquarters. There were homes for managers and supervisory personnel along Nāwiliwili Road.

Koloa Sugar, before Grove Farm bought the company, also had multiple camps such as the mill camp in Kōloa, Spanish Camp on Wailaau Road and Banana Camp (sometimes called Koloa Camp) along Waihohonu. There were also individual homes at specific locations, like the house Perfecto Labrador was raised in next to the Koloa Plantation stable. His father was the stable master.

Puhi Camp was a giant, multicultural plantation rental housing camp located mauka of the Grove Farm office, and to the western end of what is now the Kaua'i Community College campus.

Houses were generally of wood frame construction and they ranged from small to large. A very few had indoor plumbing, but most had outhouses. Agena's first home had a two-holer—an outhouse with two side-by-side seats. Often one of the holes would be smaller for children and one larger for adults. The three-bedroom home of "Bernie" (Bernadette Hanako Tokuda) Sakoda had a one-hole outhouse.

"Eventually we got an inside flush toilet and a big

Bobby Agena's first home had a two-holer—an outhouse with two side-by-side seats.

Top: Dating back to the 1880s, this home was built at Ulu Kukui for Dr. Walters. Subsequent tenants included Capt. L. Ahlborn, A.H. Smith, the Gendall family and the J.H. Moragne family. It became a girls' dormitory in the mid-1920s and was razed in 1935.
Bottom: Some of Grove Farm's skilled workers were housed in plantation-owned homes built in 1938 of hollow tile and including fireplaces. These two-bedroom homes were designed for growing plantation families; the house plan allowed for the easy addition of a third bedroom.

porcelain bathtub," Sakoda said.

Most houses had outside baths, often shared with other families. It was often a kid's job to start the fire under the *furo*-style bath to heat the water. Hard-working plantation workers would first wash, then soak in the hot wooden tub.

"The Puhi Camp community was real good," said Chick Cacabelos. "We had Filipinos, Portuguese, Japanese. We played marbles, basketball, volleyball, baseball. There was a small park in the camp."

Michiye Funaku remembers growing up in Puhi Camp with her parents and eight siblings in a four-bedroom house.

"I remember wartime. Behind our house, Grove Farm gave quite a bit of land for camp people to raise vegetables. I had to help clean the field of cane stalks. They divided the land into plots so everybody had a place to plant.

"As soon as my father came home from work he would have a few cans of beer and my mother would have something for him to eat. Then he would go work in the garden until dark. We grew cabbage, eggplant, beans, ginger, potato, *nishime* taro—everything, he planted.

"I remember soldiers asking to buy cabbages. They didn't have any fresh food," Funaku said. Her mother warned her to be careful of the soldier boys, she said.

"We had ducks and chickens, and we had rabbits for a while. I remember we had to watch out for rats. They would get under the chicken cage and bite off the feet of the chicks," Funaku said. There were other problems with rats, too.

"Before days, people would save money. You'd be surprised how much money they made, but they never keep the money in banks. One man, he had $7,000 hidden in the rafters. And the rats shredded it. He was wild, I thought he would go crazy," Labrador said.

David Nobriga's family grew corn and rice for cattle and hogs. Cacabelos recalls his family garden had "bitter melon, eggplant, *calamungay* and other Filipino things."

Diesel mechanic Perfecto Labrador started at Koloa Plantation and eventually lived for a time at Puhi Camp. He recalls that at Koloa, Filipino workers lacking garden space would plant vegetables on the *lihi*, a Hawaiian word referring to the border where soil was piled up along irrigation furrows. They would use a sharp stick to poke a hole in the soil for seeds and grew squash, pumpkin, tomatoes, sweet potato—and bitter melon grew wild.

Most workers cut their own wood for cooking

"Puhi Camp was the camp of the world!"

Bobby Agena, 70, was born into a Grove Farm family. His dad, Shiro, was a welder, and they lived in Grove Farm's Puhi Camp until they moved to the company's Pua Loke subdivision when he was twelve.

"My grandfather was a ditch man, he took care of a plantation reservoir. When my dad went looking for work, he started at Kekaha. Some plantations had work but no housing. Some had housing but no work. Grove Farm had both. He was a troubleshooter. He would go out in the fields with his welding truck and make repairs.

"I had a lot of good memories. Grove Farm took care of everybody, all the families. Every Easter there was an Easter egg hunt. There were Christmas parties," paid for by the plantation, he said.

As a boy, Bobby remembered that kids made a lot of their own toys. He remembers using a nail to make a knife, heating and hammering it to get its flat shape.

Camp life was diverse. A wide range of ethnicities. Lots of different kinds of sports. People grew some of their own food. Parts of the camp had outhouses and outdoor bathhouses with wooden furo bathtubs. Kids were assigned to build the fires to heat the water.

He remembers former-mayor Eduardo Malapit, who had lived at Puhi Camp as a boy, describing the diversity: "Puhi Camp was the camp of the world!"

Agena's family wanted something better than a rented plantation home with outdoor toilets and baths.

"My mom (Marion Panui) worked at Kaua'i Yacht Club as a waitress. She kept asking the managers to get them a house at Pua Loke until Lyle Van Dreser told her one was available." They moved into a sturdy concrete house that he recalls fondly.

Many camp kids got their first jobs working for the same plantation where their parents worked. High school kids often worked weekends and summers, cleaning up pastures, hoeing weeds, spraying weeds in the pineapple fields, picking pineapple.

"We high school kids did the work. Most of our lunas were college kids."

Robert H. "Bobby" Agena

"My dad was the 'sheriff' of the camp—he blew the whistle."

Bernie Sakoda's parents were immigrants from Okinawa and initially lived in what was called Okinawa Camp in Omao. Her grandfather was a Grove Farm laborer, and her dad, Robert Seiyei Tokuda, was a Grove Farm truck driver.

"My mother (Mitsue "Nancy" Tokuda) got Dad up early, made him breakfast and lunch and afterwards, at 6:30, she got us kids up. She worked at Puhi Store. She had all the Grove Farm employees' bango (employee numbers) memorized," Sakoda said.

Her family had been Buddhist but converted to Catholicism. Sakoda attended Catholic school and briefly attended the Immaculate Conception convent. At home, the family practiced both Buddhist and Catholic religious traditions.

Today Sakoda, 68, continues to carry on both ethnic and camp traditions. She plays her grandfather's snakeskin-covered *sanshin*, an Okinawan three-stringed instrument that looks a little like a banjo. But she also has taught Kaua'i kids to build the kind of sanshin used in camp—a *kankara* sanshin which has a large tin can as its body.

She recalled that time was counted in the camp by the Grove Farm plantation whistle, which blew several times each day, marking the start of work and the end of the work day at 3:30 p.m. The final 8 p.m. sounding marked curfew—it told every child they needed to be home.

"My dad was the 'sheriff' of the camp—he blew the whistle," Sakoda said.

"It was wonderful growing up in Puhi Camp," she said, but residents were generally thrilled to move into homes they could own—and appreciated Grove Farm's decision to build many of its subdivision homes of concrete.

"People were so happy to get out of the termite-infested homes into solid concrete homes," she said.

Sakoda went into banking and she can remember when people untrusting of banks bought their first homes using down payments from cash stored in coffee cans.

Bernadette "Bernie" Hanako Tokuda Sakoda

Top: *Some of Grove Farm's top bowlers won a trip to O'ahu in the summer of 1957. Front row, from left: Pat Agustin, Stanley Oshima, Deme Agustin, Chester Furukawa and Chick Cacabelos. Standing, from left: Henry Oshima, Taka Muraoka, Harry Hashinoto, Howard Cox, Suemi Okubo and Kazu Kurasaki.*

Above: *Wood frame houses front dirt roads at Puhi Camp in 1928. Each home has a hedge and an opening for access and an array of decorative or edible plants growing in the small yard. Family trash was burned in repurposed fifty-five-gallon oil drums, and on most plantations, company trucks emptied the ashes monthly.*

Opposite: *September 1930 blueprint of Grove Farm's Puhi Camp: In addition to houses and streets, the map shows the location of ditches, tunnels and reservoirs. Most roadways in the camp were named for trees: Cedar, Koa, Cocoanut, Palm, Pine and Algeroba (sic) Streets, among others. The Puhi Meat Market is located at bottom right, and the slaughterhouse near the laundry at top right.*

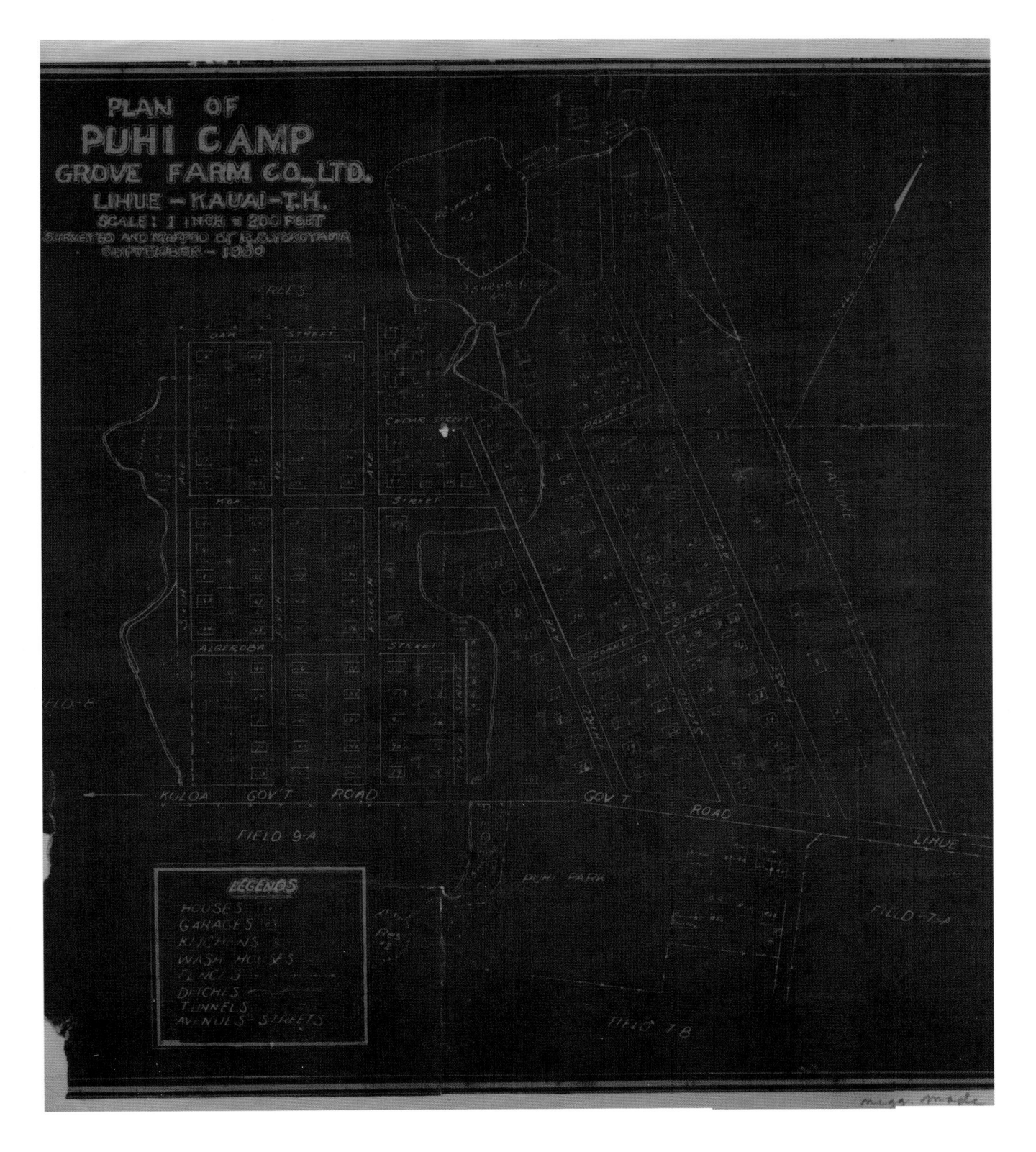

Plan of Puhi Camp, Grove Farm Co., Ltd., Lihue-Kauai-T.H. Scale: 1 inch = 200 feet. Surveyed and mapped by K. Gyokuyama, September 1930.

and water heating, but the plantation provided five gallons of kerosene per household per month. "You used kerosene when it was windy and cannot cook," Labrador said.

Animals were all over the place. Residents grew much of their own food, that included not only fruits and vegetables, but livestock. Ducks, chickens, goats, pigs and many others. Dogs and cats were also prevalent, the cats to help control the rat problem.

Potentiano "Pat" Agustin recalls wandering the abandoned Grove Farm Camp at Halehaka and reveling in the fruit trees that grew there: lychee, star apple, cream apple or momona, vi apple, mango and banana. He was also impressed by the graveyards around the Halehaka site where there were both Japanese and Chinese residential camps.

Another valley over toward Kīpū was called by the kids "Fruit Valley," Bobby Agena said.

"It was past the shops toward Kīpū. Grove Farm grew all kinds of fruit. We would go and pick mango, lychee. We roamed the whole area. They never used to close us out. We would walk up through pastures to Kukaua, the 'White House'—we had names for all the places—we would go up by Lonely Tree and eat ratberry (also known as downy rose myrtle). We had slingshots. We made popguns with bamboo and we blew bubbles with papaya leaf stalks," Agena said.

"We were very creative," said Bernie Sakoda. Those who were skilled with slingshots would shoot small birds, which the kids would eat.

"We ate doves, *mejiro*. We would put them on the water heater fire to cook them," Sakoda said.

Residents of plantation camps could get a lot of their food and other goods delivered without having to go to the store. The stores often sent salesmen out to collect orders, and would deliver the goods the same afternoon.

"Koji Kuboyama would come to our house to take orders," Bernie Sakoda remembers.

There was a family in Līhu'e that made tofu and sold it in the camp.

"We had the tofu lady come from Līhu'e with

GROWING UP GROVE FARM 69

tofu in two five-gallon cracker cans she carried on a stick over her shoulder," Sakoda said. And on Sundays, Mr. Akau would arrive to sell manju.

"He would come with a weird-looking wagon, selling all the Chinese delicacies. 'Manju, manapua, pepeiao,' he would yell," she said.

In a time before television and personal electronics, when they weren't out exploring, "We played all kinds of games," said Bobby Agena. There were open fields available for group sporting activities, and kids would create makeshift playing sites in the dirt for marbles competitions. Kids participated in baseball, softball, volleyball, boxing, tennis and more.

Agustin recalls traveling to Honolulu for high school sporting activities. And occasionally, the camp workers would compete with workers from other plantations. Chick Cacabelos recalls that among other sports, he took up tennis.

"Me and Pat Agustin went to play Lihue Plantation. We're these two short Filipinos, but we gave them good competition," he said.

And there were, of course, non-athletic sporting activities, notably cockfighting.

"Everybody raised chickens for fighting. Fights were multicultural, although Filipinos, mostly. Fights were generally on Sundays and they were done by 3 p.m. The food at the chicken fights was the best," Sakoda said.

Chick Cacabelos recalls that his earliest involvement in chicken fighting was cooking the roosters that lost. His first job was to be in charge of boiling water to prepare the losing chickens for the pot.

Later he raised fighting chickens and fought them, earning his Filipino nickname "Manok," which means chicken, as well as his English nickname, "Chick." He says he gave up fighting and eventually only raised chickens for food.

There were other entirely or somewhat illegal activities going on around plantation camps, generally without the approval of the plantation.

Labrador recalls that his father was the "Al Capone" of Koloa Plantation—a bootlegger during Prohibition who manufactured beer and Java plum wine in a brewery hidden in the cane fields. He was able to make beer using barley from horse feed since he worked in the plantation stable. And his sugar purchases were explained by his wife's baking of confections.

"All the camp single men would buy it at twenty-five cents for a big bottle," Labrador said.

"Once, the federal officers came to search our house. They looked all over the house but they found nothing. To age it, the wine was under the house, covered with bags and dirt," he said. His family had a secret door in the house floor, which allowed access to the spirits hidden below.

The illicit making of alcohol wasn't new to the Islands. George Norton Wilcox referred to the distillation of alcohol from ti root back in the 1800s.

"Once when we were looking for distilleries which had flourished under Tom Marshall, we came across an imu with four fine ti roots in it. Perhaps you will see baked ti root sometimes in the market now. But none could ever taste as that did. You know a few hours did not do for ti root—they would leave it in for two or even three days and then it was good! My, I wish I had one now," Wilcox said in an oral history that is housed at Grove Farm Homestead Museum.

Michiye Funaku remembers that Grove Farm *okolehao* was still being produced, quietly, in the 1950s and '60s, during the period when ti root was being processed for its levulose content.

"Now and then a bottle would appear at the Grove Farm office," she said. 🌿

Above: *Koloa Store reopens with new merchandising displays after a 1948 remodeling.*
Opposite, top left: *Mitsugi Nishihara and Caesar Vasconcelles peruse the merchandise.*
Opposite, bottom left: *Behind the counter, Naoki Muronaka and Alexander Ruiz wait on Mrs. Herman Brandt.*
Opposite, right: *(left to right) Yuhie Sanekane, Charles Furukawa, Vincente Bargo and Saturnino Racelo at the Koloa Store in 1949.*

GROWING UP GROVE FARM 71

By the 1970s, sugar was no longer the big-money crop it had been. Here, the final harvest marks the close of operations at Koloa Mill.

Chapter 5
The Troubles

"(G.N. Wilcox) was always a cautious operator and did not like to borrow money."
—Gaylord P. Wilcox

"We borrowed $35 million... Then the Gulf War came along, and Hurricane Iniki—who could have predicted that? And nothing sold. We had no income to pay off the loan."
—former Grove Farm president David Pratt

It had long been clear that Grove Farm's independence, while it provided benefits like flexibility, also put the company at risk—particularly in those years when low world sugar prices, labor strikes or hurricanes significantly depressed income.

Most other sugar plantations in the Islands had reduced the risk of being small and solitary by becoming part of larger corporate conglomerates. On Kaua'i, by the 1970s, for example, Lihue Plantation and Kekaha Sugar were part of Amfac. Kilauea Sugar and Olokele Sugar were part of C. Brewer. McBryde Sugar was part of Alexander & Baldwin. Each of these parent companies also had plantations on other islands.

In Hawai'i, only Grove Farm and Gay & Robinson remained independent and largely family-owned sugar operations. And sugar was not the big-money crop it had once been. Sugar prices had not kept pace with costs of production and labor costs were the highest in the world.

In the Grove Farm annual report for 1970, president and CEO Sam Wilcox wrote about his family company's vulnerability:

"Standing on our own, without an agency company's financial backing in poor sugar years, we must have proper diversification to take up the slack. Fortunately in 1970 our strong cash position saw us through. However, this may not always be the case and your management and directors are continually looking for some profitable diversification within our means to finance."

It was a policy of diversification that dates right back to George N. Wilcox, who began investing outside his plantation as soon as he began making money—in steamships, other sugar plantations, a guano fertilizer endeavor and crops that were alternatives to sugar.

Under Sam Wilcox, one means the company was already employing was leveraging its construction crews' expertise and its land holdings to begin developing subdivisions.

Grove Farm had always built housing for its employees, the difference being that the first projects were rentals. The company built and owned the housing, and either let employees live there free or for minimal rental amounts.

"I can remember the first Japanese who were brought in for Grove Farm and G.N. building enough houses to take care of them in Halehaka Valley. He also had, lower down in the valley, another camp in which he housed Chinese," said Gaylord P. Wilcox.

There were other camps scattered around Grove Farm land built back when workers walked or rode horses to work, and lived near the fields they tilled or the other workplaces where they toiled.

"Originally the people who worked on the plantation lived in several villages in the valleys. As the plantation grew, G.N. decided he had better start new headquarters and he selected the area on the edge of the Puhi Valley for a village for employees and built houses as fast as possible," Gaylord Wilcox said.

That was Puhi Camp, and it would serve Grove Farm's multicultural workforce for decades. But then the company began looking at getting out of the rental business. At both Kōloa, where there were still several plantation camps, and at Puhi, the company began developing housing for sale.

Initially, they were aimed at providing low-cost housing to Grove Farm employees as the company began getting out of the employee rental housing business. Eventually, that development expertise would be turned to selling subdivision lots to the general public. But it did not evolve into the profit center that sugar had once been.

The company had a major rock quarrying

> **Sugar prices had not kept pace with costs of production and labor costs were the highest in the world.**

Top and Bottom: *Grove Farm's policy of diversification dated back to the days of G.N. Wilcox, who began investing in diversified agriculture early on. One of the company's alternative crops to sugar was pineapple. Here in 1945, a Grove Farm pineapple harvester operates in the shadow of the Hā'upu Range, with ten workers in a line following an extended boom and conveyor system. The pineapple harvester was designed by W.M. Moragne and built in the Grove Farm shop.*

division. Grove Farm's rock quarries at Halfway Bridge, Māhāʻulepū and Kīlauea provided virtually all of the island's rock supplies for construction and road building. The company increased the capacity of its rock quarries to meet the requirements of the growing island community. It amounted to a quarter of Grove Farm's revenues in some years, but it was still not enough to provide financial stability to the firm.

"You were just skating along, breaking even most of the time. From the late '60s, we realized we weren't getting anywhere. When sugar prices were high, you used the money to buy equipment that you couldn't afford when prices were low," said David W. Pratt, who joined the company from Amfac Sugar in 1972 and became Grove Farm president and CEO in 1974, succeeding Sam Wilcox.

In its review of its options, Grove Farm began talking to its sugar-growing neighbors, Lihue Plantation to the north and McBryde to the west. Would either be interested in gaining economies of scale in their operations by adding Grove Farm's sugar lands to their own? Both expressed initial interest, but as negotiations proceeded, they went slowly and it was difficult to see how it would get to a conclusion.

Which neighboring plantation would take which acreage and how would the operations be merged? "It took two years to negotiate that," Pratt said. "At one point near the end, we were negotiating with Eddie Holyroyde of A&B and Karl Berg of Amfac. Eventually, Eddie said, 'We'll take the whole thing.' Karl said no. And that broke the dam toward making a deal."

In a complex arrangement, Amfac would lease 2,800 acres of Grove Farm land north of the Haʻupu mountain range, and McBryde/A&B would take the remaining acreage on the other side of the mountain, along with the mill. The McBryde portion included both Grove Farm-owned land and parts of the sugar plantation that Grove Farm had leased from the Knudsen Estate.

The deal was completed in January 1974, with McBryde leasing 7,200 acres of Grove Farm's plantation to bring its acreage to 13,163, and Lihue Plantation taking 2,800 to bring its total to 17,500.

There remained a laundry list of issues.

The most convenient route between Grove Farm's Koloa lands and McBryde's sugar fields was owned by a trust of the Knudsen family. "We worked out a land exchange with Valdemar Knudsen for a haul-cane right of way from Koloa lands to McBryde lands. Grove Farm still owns that road," Pratt said.

McBryde would get the 2.5-billion-gallon Waitā Reservoir and all its immense irrigation capacity. But McBryde argued that the Waitā dam needed repairs. Grove Farm arranged for engineering and construction to refurbish Waitā's dam. (The name Waitā for what once was the Kōloa Reservoir has a provenance that's not well understood. *Place Names of Hawaii* suggests it should be written Waitā, and that it may be from Hawaiian *wai* for water and Japanese *ta* for rice paddy.)

Unique leasing arrangements were created on a parcel-by-parcel basis in some cases. To avoid triggering prohibitive subdivision laws, company attorney Daniel Case recommended dividing up one large agricultural parcel this way: McBryde would lease the entire parcel and Lihue Plantation would also lease the entire parcel. And then each of them would agree to the exclusive use by the other of a designated portion of the property.

Top: *Growing sugar at Grove Farm in 1890 meant using innovative irrigation systems. Note the ditch system at lower right.*
Bottom: *Workers inspect cane in 1949.*

THE TROUBLES 75

At Puhi in the 1950s, with the sugar industry still in its heyday, Grove Farm's impressive inventory of rolling stock and field equipment is flanked by a thriving community of employee homes. Opposite: The same view today shows Kaua'i Community College at upper right and part of the company's industrial and residential subdivisions.

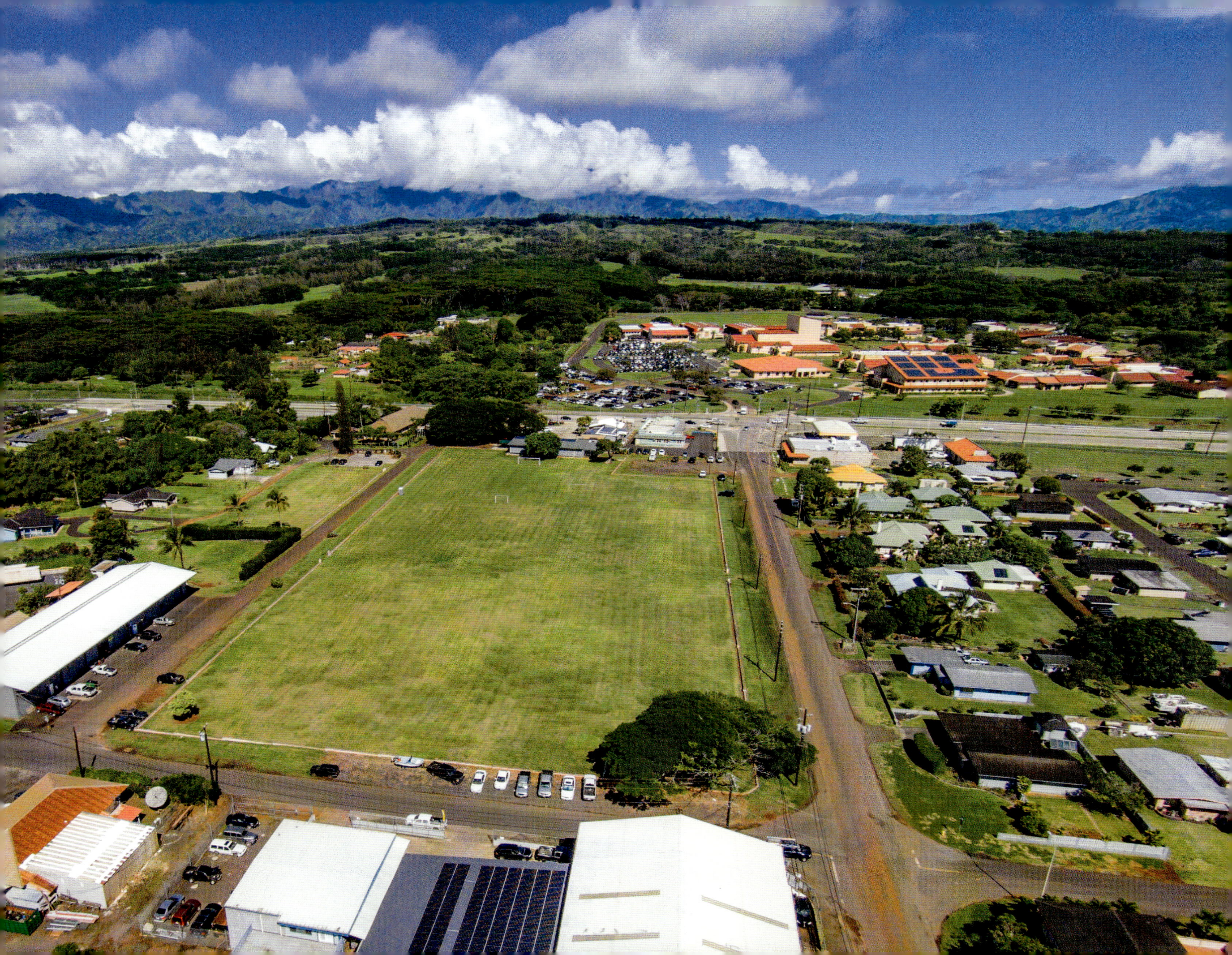

Viewed in the opposite direction (see previous pages), fields of cane still stretch beyond Grove Farm's industrial yard in the 1950s. Opposite: Today, the cane has been replaced by an industrial park and residential communities.

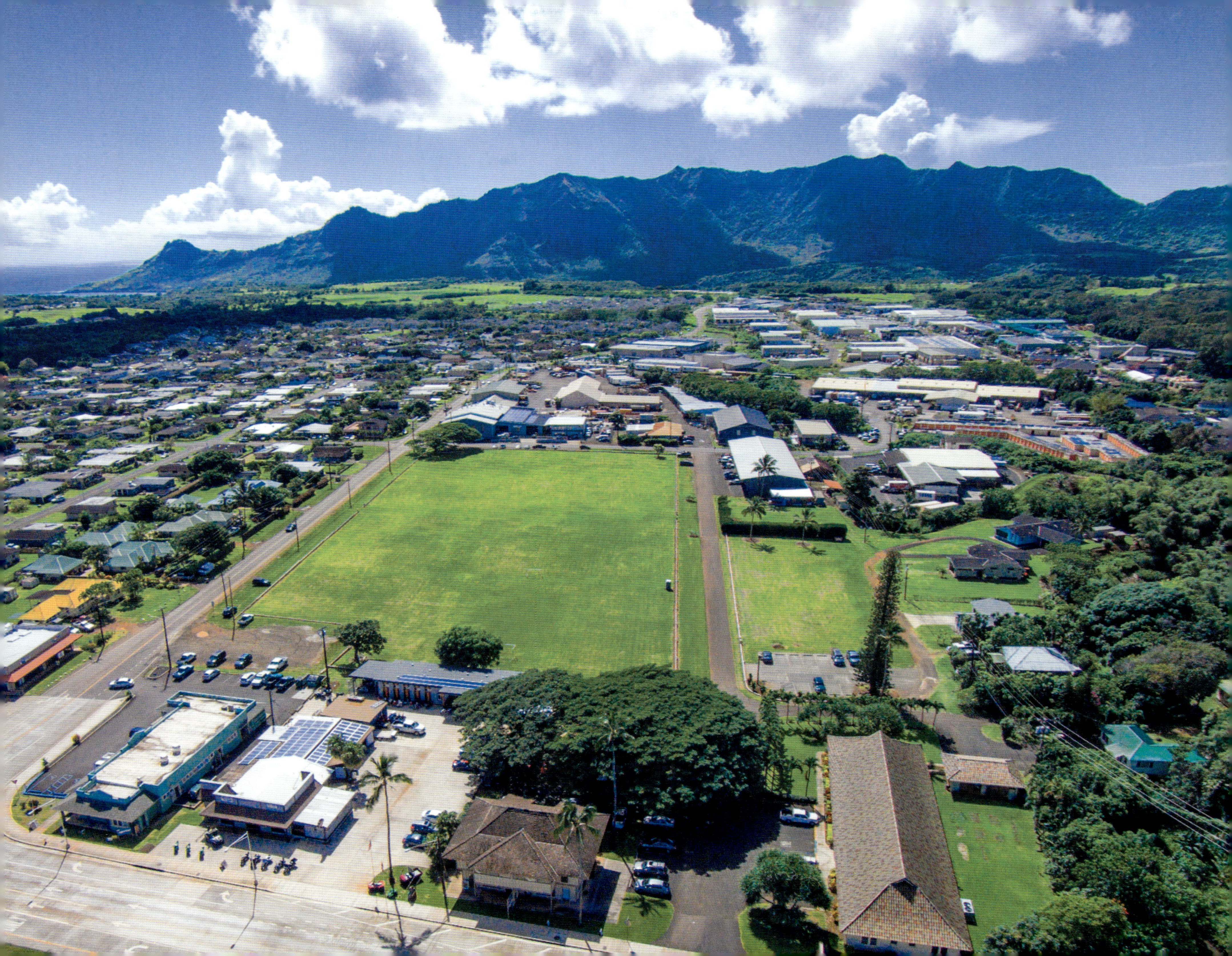

Dividing up the employees was another issue. Some went to McBryde and some to Lihue. Some took early retirement. A very few were left without work. "Almost everybody got a job that wanted one," Pratt said.

Once the details were complete, Grove Farm was out of the sugar business for the first time in 110 years. Grove Farm would receive a base lease rental every year, plus a portion of profits.

"The good news was that we made money in every year. We could have a regular dividend. That worked out really well," Pratt said.

But it raised a new issue for the company, said Dan Case. "There was a question of what to do." Steve Case has studied the company and its history, and recognizes the quandary Grove Farm's principals were in.

"We are recognizing that businesses have to reinvent themselves. Grove Farm has tried to do that. David Pratt is a good example, realizing thirty years ago that continued focus on sugar was not going to be a good model. Opportunity in ag was disappearing," he said.

The company began converting itself from an agricultural firm to a land management company. One thing it had considered was the need for a regional shopping complex or some commercial or retail project on its lands. In anticipation of that, in 1975 the company arranged a cash-and-land-swap deal in which it acquired from Lihue Plantation a forty-acre parcel at the major intersection of Kaumuali'i Highway and Nāwiliwili Road.

"It was a major intersection and it was an outlying parcel for Lihue Plantation. It seemed like a perfect place for some kind of development," Pratt said.

Pratt remembers a critical moment four years later when Grove Farm learned that Honolulu financier Harry Weinberg was proposing to build a shopping center on Rice Street property he owned. Some of the major likely tenants including Liberty House and Longs Drugs approached Grove Farm to ask if it was planning to build and expressed interest in leasing. Weinberg had a fearsome reputation as a hard bargainer and the tenants hoped that they would have an easier time dealing with Grove Farm, he said.

Pratt said Grove Farm had little actual planning done, but felt it faced a critical situation. If Weinberg went forward, it might preclude Grove Farm from developing its lands to the south of Nāwiliwili Valley. So Grove Farm asserted to county planners that it indeed intended to build a shopping center and quickly acquired development consultants. They were veterans Egan Nishimoto and Stanley Tabata. Pratt said he trusted his consultants since his own credentials in development were weak. He was a sugar farmer by training.

"I didn't know (much). I was an ag guy," he said. But he was learning fast. There were unexpected decisions to make. The property for the shopping center sloped sixty feet from highest to lowest location. Should the project pay more in grading costs to create an entirely flat shopping center, or save some money by having it on two levels with

> "We are recognizing that businesses have to reinvent themselves. Grove Farm has tried to do that."

stairs connecting them? "We decided that stairs were a psychological barrier, and to pay extra to avoid that," he said.

"It was a big project and it was a scary period. Interest rates were over twenty percent on the construction loan. But with our early anchors—Liberty House, Longs, Sears and Star Market—the project carried itself."

Top and Bottom: *Historically Grove Farm had leveraged its construction crews' skills with outside jobs. In 1939, its carpenters built the Immaculate Conception Church in Kapaia with hollow tile made at the company's tile plant. Today this Roman Catholic church serves the Līhu'e, Hanamā'ulu and Puhi communities.*

And since some of the anchors had approached Grove Farm to develop the center, Grove Farm called on them to help pay for some of the improvements upfront. Even so, the center was a big expense for Grove Farm.

Case, the company's attorney at the time, said it was a daunting project. "It was logical, but it was a significant financial challenge from the debt they took on. That shopping center (Kukui Grove Center) was a major development for a small company," Case said.

In 1982, Hurricane Iwa caused significant damage to the brand new shopping center and depressed the island's economy for several years thereafter, making it difficult to run a retail operation like a shopping center.

At the same time, Grove Farm was picking up the pace of developing housing. The company had sold 338 mostly house-and-lot packages, mostly to employees, from 1950 to 1971. In the next two decades, it developed and sold more than 500 more; most of them developed lots sold to the general public.

But the cost and time involved in repeatedly seeking county and state zoning approvals for individual projects were weighing the company down.

"We decided, rather than go back to the Planning Commission over and over, to have Belt Collins & Associates develop a master plan. To add to Grove Farm's shopping center, the Līhu'e-Puhi master plan identified locations for additional housing, industrial uses and recreational facilities like an eighteen-hole golf course.

In 1987, Pratt brought in sugar executive Allan Smith, with whom he had worked at Amfac, and who knew Grove Farm lands well as the field superintendent for Lihue Plantation. Smith had both a general contractors' license and a real estate license.

"I came to Grove Farm as vice president and operations manager, with responsibility for the quarry, construction, the shop—everything except the shopping center," Smith recalls.

Then came a series of significant setbacks.

"There was so much turmoil."

Remy Chinen had a front row seat on nearly a half-century of Grove Farm's history, starting as a clerk typist and eventually becoming the company's executive secretary and corporate secretary.

She was born in early 1942 in Ilocos Sur in the Philippines. Her dad, working as an irrigator with Lihue Plantation, brought the family to Hawai'i in 1946, where they lived in plantation housing in Hanamā'ulu. After attending Hanamaulu School and Kauai High School, she went to Kauai Technical School, then joined a training program at Grove Farm as a clerk typist in 1962, when the company had just closed its pineapple and cattle ranching operations.

"At first I was apprehensive, because it was all haoles I was working for. But Grove Farm was a family company; it was family-oriented. Employees came to the office with their problems. It was comfortable to be in the office. People were so warm, so much aloha," she said.

"I answered phones, picked up the mail, and transcribed (dictated) letters. I worked with the executive secretary, Ms. Gladys Butler." Chinen, who had married in 1965, was elevated to executive secretary in 1977 and in 1986 to corporate secretary, which meant she sat in on all meetings of the board of directors.

Chinen clearly remembers the period when Grove Farm went out of sugar, leasing its fields to McBryde and Lihue Plantation.

"There was so much turmoil," she said, "but the company took care of most of the employees." (Many took new positions with the other plantations.)

There was difficulty in the boardroom, too, as directors accustomed to running a farming company were forced to make the transition to a land management and development company.

When the company ran into severe financial trouble and massive layoffs were enacted, Chinen was asked if she wanted to stay on.

"It was 1998. It was an honor and a privilege to have worked for Grove Farm Company—it was an experience of a lifetime. I had an option to stay. But I was thinking about the younger generation. If I stayed, one of them would have to go. The company gave me a good package and I took it," she said.

Chinen stayed peripherally connected to the Grove Farm legacy with a ten-year part-time stint at Grove Farm Homestead Museum before she fully retired.

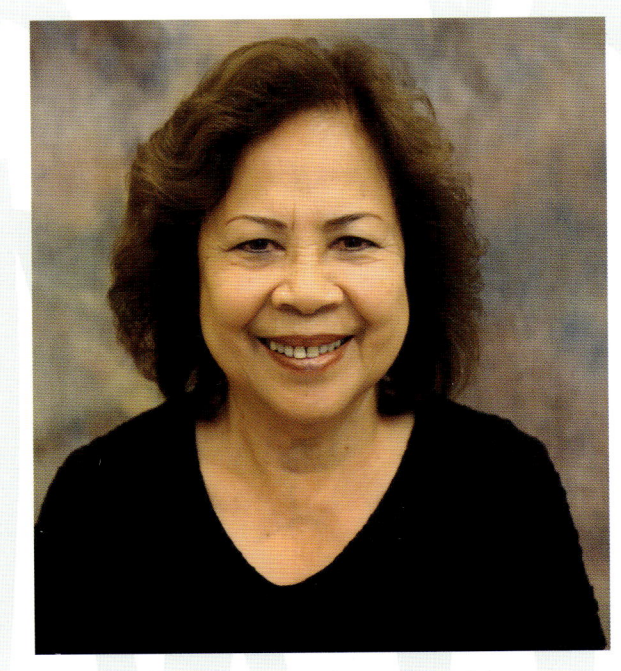

Remedios "Remy" Alayvilla Chinen

"A steep learning curve..."

Like many Grove Farm employees, David W. Pratt had a family history with the company. Pratt, 79, is the grandson of former Grove Farm manager E.H.W. "Ned" Broadbent and the son of former Grove Farm corporate attorney Dudley Pratt Sr. He started his sugar industry career with Amfac plantations. But he was called to Grove Farm in 1972 by his father-in-law, Sam Wilcox, who was then president.

He was a sugar executive, but had come to Grove Farm at the very time it was shutting down its own sugar operations and leasing its cane land to adjacent plantations.

Pratt became president of Grove Farm in 1975, as the company was converting itself to a land management and development company. Pratt concedes that he was on a steep learning curve. He knew sugar cane. He didn't know much about development.

For much of his time at the company Pratt was overseeing Grove Farm's new housing projects in Līhu'e, Puhi and Kōloa. Many of them were aimed at getting current or former Grove Farm employees out of company-owned rental housing and into homes they could own.

His first major project was the Kukui Grove Shopping Center, the biggest venture Grove Farm had ever attempted. The company borrowed heavily to pay for it, but leases covered the payments, Pratt said.

In the early '80s, Pratt hired the planning and engineering firm Belt Collins to prepare a master plan for development of 600 acres of the company's lands around Līhu'e and Puhi.

In a case of deeply unfortunate timing, Grove Farm, still paying off the shopping center mortgage, borrowed another $35 million for its Līhu'e-Puhi projects just before the first Gulf War and Hurricane Iniki. Those events caused a significant and extended recession on Kaua'i. The company eventually lacked the cash to make its loan payments.

As financial woes increased, Pratt retired in March 1996 rather than lay off most of Grove Farm's employees. That task was handed to his successor, Guido Giacometti, and later Hugh Klebahn.

Once Steve Case bought Grove Farm from the Wilcox family, Pratt was asked to resume the company's leadership. He was president the second time from January 2001 to February 2005.

David W. Pratt

When Grove Farm went to the State Land Use Commission, the commission required that sixty percent of the homes be "affordable." For Grove Farm, that meant houses developed and sold at less than it cost to build them.

"We made a deal with Schuler (housing developer Schuler Homes) to do the affordable housing," Pratt recalled. "We sold them the land, but with our infrastructure improvements, it cost more than we got."

Then Grove Farm made a critical—in retrospect—decision about its major Līhu'e-Puhi project. It decided that costs would not be going down so it seemed to make sense to immediately build streets, wastewater and other utilities. It started the roads and wastewater plant, the Puakea Golf Course, commercial lots and house lots along the golf course.

"We borrowed $35 million to build it. Then the Gulf War came along and Hurricane Iniki—who could have predicted that? And nothing sold. We had no income to pay off the loan," Pratt said. Smith recalls that another key decision was Grove Farm's decision to try to ensure long-term cash flow by not selling commercial lands. It decided it would lease them instead. "It's Monday morning quarterbacking, but if we'd sold the fee, we would have been all right," he said, since the sales would have provided large chunks of cash that could have paid down debt.

Many of Grove Farm's shareholders, while they were Wilcox family members, lived on the Mainland and had limited connection to the Islands outside of their stock in Grove Farm. Dan Case said some of them depended on regularly receiving their Grove Farm dividends, and grew restive when the economic downturn and significant debts cut off the shareholder checks.

Steve Case said he recognizes the issue with widely distributed ownership.

"It is, at one level, a nice thing to do to distribute shares but if you distribute it over lots of people and multiple generations, that's lots of people with a variety of different views and that leads to dissension," he said. "What really created the problem at Grove Farm was when the hurricane and the economy conspired to halt the limited investment they could make, leading to things getting pretty dire."

In addition to unhappy shareholders, Pratt and the board had lender issues. The company was falling behind on its mortgages and major banks holding Grove Farm debt—First Hawaiian Bank and Bank of Hawaiʻi—were demanding payment. One insisted Grove Farm identify additional collateral for its loan.

"Given these market conditions, your company's financial condition has deteriorated," Pratt wrote in the 1995 annual report.

"It got worse and worse," Case said. The company was aggressively cutting costs. Employees were placed on a thirty-two-hour workweek. Early retirements were encouraged. Dividends were suspended. Directors' fees were cut. But it wasn't enough. The board decided the company needed to lay off significant numbers of its employees. Pratt opted to retire, in part to avoid being the hatchet man, and in part, he said, to hand the reins to someone with more development experience.

For its next president and CEO, the board turned to Grove Farm board member Guido Giacometti, a respected Hawaiʻi real estate professional. Smith was tasked with making the job cuts. "There was excess cash in the pension fund and we used that to pay severance. Not one person spat on my shoes," Smith said. When he had arrived at the company, it had about 125 employees, he recalls. By the time the purges were done, the count was in the neighborhood of a dozen employees.

Giacometti renegotiated the company's debt with First Hawaiian Bank. Pratt said that was an important advance in the company's situation, although it ultimately was not sufficient.

Right: Homes at Puhi Camp (1930 plan drawn up by assistant manager and later manager William Moragne) had been rented to Grove Farm employees for decades, but by the 1950s the company was beginning to get out of the rental business.

THE TROUBLES 83

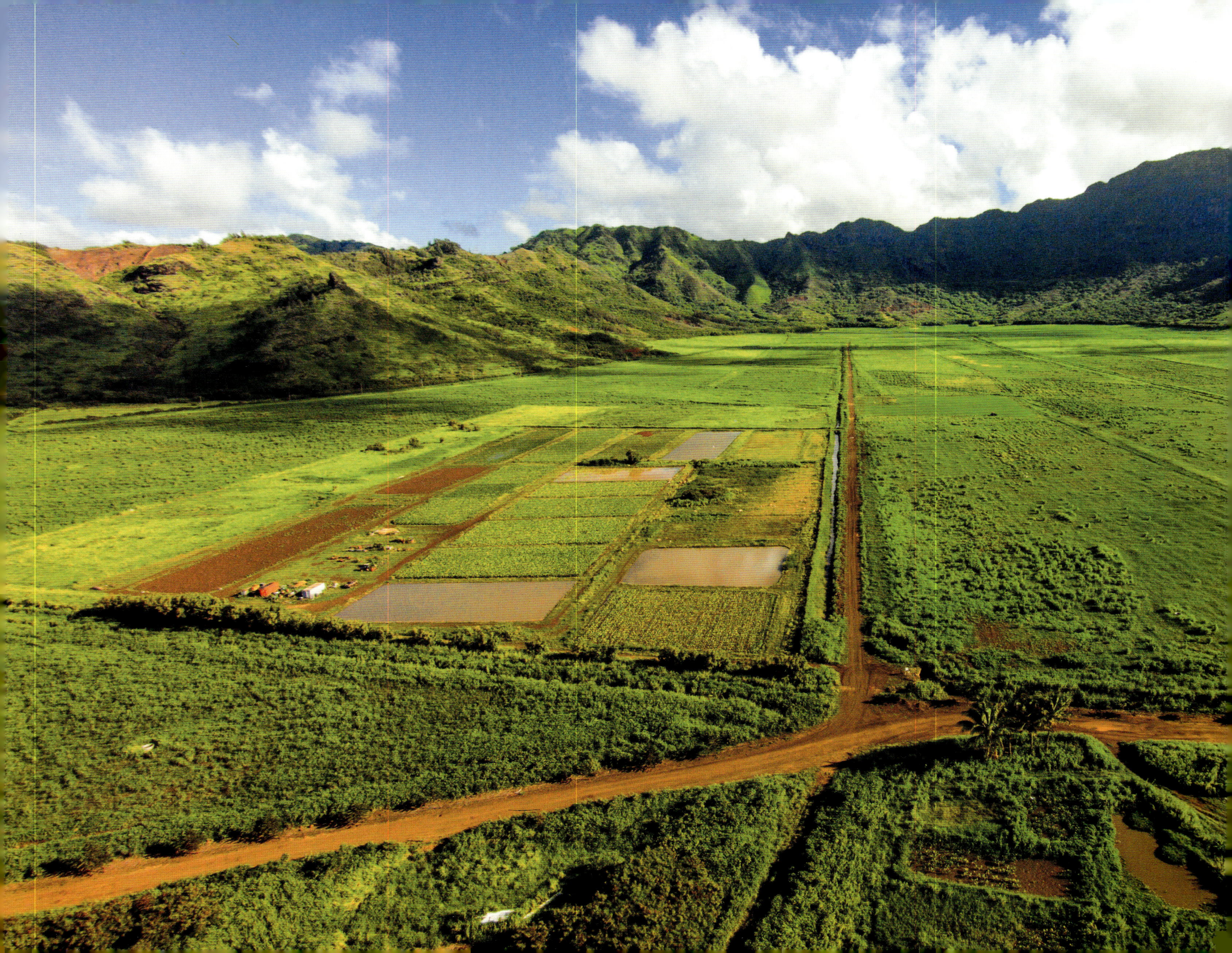

Significant upgrades were needed at the shopping center, but there were so many retail vacancies that without new tenants, the company would not be able to recover the cost of the improvements. The company's audited financial statements were delayed for 1996 due to restructuring and bank negotiations.

In the 1996 annual report, for the first time both the president/CEO and the chairman of the board of directors signed the opening letter. "It was," said Giacometti and board chairman Hugh Klebahn, "a difficult year."

Despite the dramatic cost cutting, the company reported a net loss of $11.1 million. To prop up its cash flow, in spite of the weak real estate market, the company resorted to identifying and selling properties "not required to further its business."

Grove Farm kept anticipating improvement, but economic conditions failed to improve. The company managed to reduce its loss in 1997, but still was $4.4 million in the red. Giacometti left and Klebahn adopted the joint role of board chair and CEO. He began searching for an investment partner who might be able to insert new capital to keep Grove Farm alive.

"Management moved aggressively during the second half of the year (of 1998) to posture the company as an asset manager and to discontinue all insignificant operations," Klebahn wrote in the 1998 annual report.

The company sold its rock crusher to Jas. W. Glover Ltd. It turned over management of the shopping center, and its sewer and water company to management by the real estate firm Chaney Brooks. It was looking to sell undeveloped bulk parcels of land. Employment at Grove Farm would be down to eight by mid-1999.

In 1998, Grove Farm eked out a profit of $1.3 million, but only by halting paying for employee and retirement medical plans—which saved the company $3.4 million. Klebahn was for the first time hopeful: "It is now apparent from our budgets that the company can survive in its reorganized form."

But by the next year, stark reality had sunk back in. The company lost $5.3 million and was looking at an immediate need of more than $8 million in cash to make loan payments to banks, make termite damage repairs at the shopping center and do work on its water system. It was cash Grove Farm didn't have and had no realistic expectation of borrowing. Smith said it might have been possible to sell off large pieces of Grove Farm land, but that was something the majority of shareholders said they did not want. They wanted to keep the family company whole to the degree possible. Besides, real estate was still depressed—part of a decade-long slump that followed 1992's Hurricane Iniki.

The company's crippling debt to First Hawaiian and Bank of Hawai'i exceeded $62 million. Klebahn wrote: "The task ahead...continues to be difficult because of the company's highly leveraged position, general economic conditions and the real estate market on Kaua'i."

Dan Case said the board was realistically considering three options to avoid losing the company to the banks: Selling Grove Farm off in pieces and hoping there was something left once the indebtedness was paid off, although many family members opposed this; seeking an investor willing to partner even though this could significantly reduce future dividends to shareholders; and selling the company whole.

The first inkling of the future came in December 1999, when chairman Hugh Klebahn's son-in-law Scott A. Blum offered to buy Grove Farm outright for $125 a share, a $21 million offer. 🌺

Opposite: *Diversified agriculture 2014: Flooded taro paddies lie surrounded by Hawaii Dairy Farms pastureland under development in Grove Farm's Māhā'ulepū Valley. The valley was once a rich sugar cane growing area for Grove Farm.*

Steve Case's vast Kaua'i holdings at one point encompassed nearly 40,000 acres, of which 22,000 were in the original Grove Farm acquisition.

Chapter 6
Selling Grove Farm

"When I first did it, there was no clear plan. It was just buying an asset that hopefully would be more valuable down the road. But it was always viewed as a mix of profit and purpose." —Steve Case

"Instead of investing in land in Florida, I suggested land in Hawai'i. It would tie him to Hawai'i. He never saw the land [as an adult] until after the sale." —Dan Case

Grove Farm owned nearly 22,000 acres of Kaua'i land, including five miles of oceanfront property, the island's largest shopping center and a golf course surrounded by developable property—and it was inches from bankruptcy.

The first angel to show up was Scott Blum, whose fortune was built on founding the Internet retailer Buy.com. He was the son-in-law of Grove Farm board chair Hugh Klebahn, and his $125 per share offer was contingent on the approval of at least seventy-five percent of Grove Farm stockholders. Because of the family conflict of interest, Klebahn stepped away from the negotiations and a special board committee was established to handle the offer. The special committee's members were Randolph G. Moore, who was elected chair, and Donn A. Carswell, Pamela W. Dohrman, Robert D. Mullins, Wilcox Patterson and William D. Pratt. On January 21, 2000, stockholders met and voted two-thirds in favor of selling to Blum—but short of the seventy-five percent he required.

However, when polled, eighty-eight percent said they might sell if the terms were right, and the special board committee was tasked with looking into alternatives. Three companies stepped forward to express interest in acquiring Grove Farm. The special committee hired the consulting firm Aspen Venture Group to advise the board.

Aspen studied alternatives available to the board and recommended that sale of the whole company was the best option. It said a fair market value was between $86 and $98 a share, significantly less than what had been offered.

The committee reopened discussion with Blum, but also talked with Honolulu bidder Honu Group, which offered $130 per share and then $136 per share and then $140. There were also other bidders in the mix. Blum dropped out during the year 2000, removing Klebahn's potential conflict of interest, and the special committee handed the negotiations

Left: *Five miles of oceanfront property, including beautiful Māhā'ulepū Beach, represent one of Grove Farm's most valuable assets.*

back to the full board.

David Pratt, who was off the board but remained a stockholder, recalls that each of the bids had contingencies or other complexities that made it difficult to directly compare them. Court documents indicate that some included mixtures of cash and land, or proposed deals in which some Grove Farm stockholders could remain stockholders in the surviving company. One or more of the bidders could not show the financial resources to actually complete the purchase.

In the case of Honu, court documents show that after the financial firm Lehman Brothers sent Grove Farm a letter indicating it was not in a joint venture with Honu to buy Grove Farm, the board required additional evidence of Honu's ability to finance the acquisition. Eventually, Honu's offer expired. And one thing that was clear to the board: Grove Farm desperately needed an infusion of hard cash by the end of the year 2000 just to keep the company afloat.

On September 19, 2000, Dan Case suggested that his son, Internet pioneer Steve Case, might be interested in making an offer. The younger Case's fortune, like Blum's, had an Internet basis. He was a founder of AOL, which earlier in 2000 had merged with Time Warner in a $164 billion deal. In September 2000, Steve Case was still awaiting Federal Trade Commission approval of the purchase as his representatives negotiated the purchase of Grove Farm.

"I had no idea if Steve would be interested, but I asked Hugh (Klebahn) if he would like me to ask Steve to make an offer. He jumped at it. The offers were not going well," Dan Case said. "I contacted Steve around September. He had mentioned something about investing in land in Florida, and I said, 'Why not do it in a place you know?'"

Dan Case was Grove Farm's corporate counsel and his firm, Case Bigelow & Lombardi, represented Grove Farm. Case sought and received a waiver of

---

Right: Grove Farm's headquarters office was built in Puhi when the company outgrew its two-room wood frame office. *Above:* The original office (green roof on far right) still stands today adjacent to a vast lawn at Grove Farm Homestead Museum, surrounded by fruit, timber and ornamental trees collected by George Norton Wilcox.

"A yard big enough for football..."

Daniel H. Case was born in 1925 and raised on Grove Farm Plantation. Case's grandfather was the county attorney and later territorial judge on Maui. His father, Aderial Hebard "Hib" Case, arrived at Grove Farm about 1918 with agriculture schooling and started as a supervisor, or luna, on the plantation. But Hib Case soon became George N. Wilcox's bookkeeper and office manager, and eventually chief financial officer of Grove Farm.

Dan Case was the youngest of three boys in the family. Oldest brother Jim Case became a prominent Honolulu attorney, as did Dan Case himself. Middle brother Bill Case started in the sugar business with C. Brewer & Co. and worked there for his entire career, first as a trainee and later as the manager of many Hawai'i plantations until his ultimate retirement. On Kaua'i, the Case family lived in company-owned homes along Nāwiliwili Road—ending up in the manager's home that had been built by Henry Digby Sloggett.

"I have all happy memories of those days," Dan Case recalled. "Our neighbors were the Alexander boys. The manager's house was the playground for everybody, with tennis, a swimming pool and a yard big enough for football. Papalinahoa had these massive mangoes. We would get mountain apples from the Gap.

"We would spend a week in summer at the YMCA's Camp Naue, and sometimes we would stay at the Alexander's mountain house in Kōke'e, or Mabel Wilcox would let us use her beach house at Po'ipū. We probably spent five or six hours a day in the water. We hiked up and down that entire coastline."

Like other Līhu'e kids, whether the children of managers or mechanics or ditch men, the Case boys went to Lihue Grammar School, where the Kaua'i Department of Water offices are now. Case went on to Punahou School, served in the U.S. Navy and then attended law school, arriving back in the Islands in 1952.

He joined the law firm headed by Dudley Pratt Sr., who was Grove Farm's attorney. When Dudley Pratt retired, he passed the Grove Farm account on to Case.

Daniel H. Case

Taro is one of many diversified food crops now produced in partnerships with small growers on Grove Farm land.

The vast Waitā Reservoir lies between Koloa Mill (opposite bottom) and Kāhili Peak. Much of the reservoir's water was once carried by ditch and tunnel around the Hā'upu Range (far right), but is now brought in by tunnel under the mountain range.

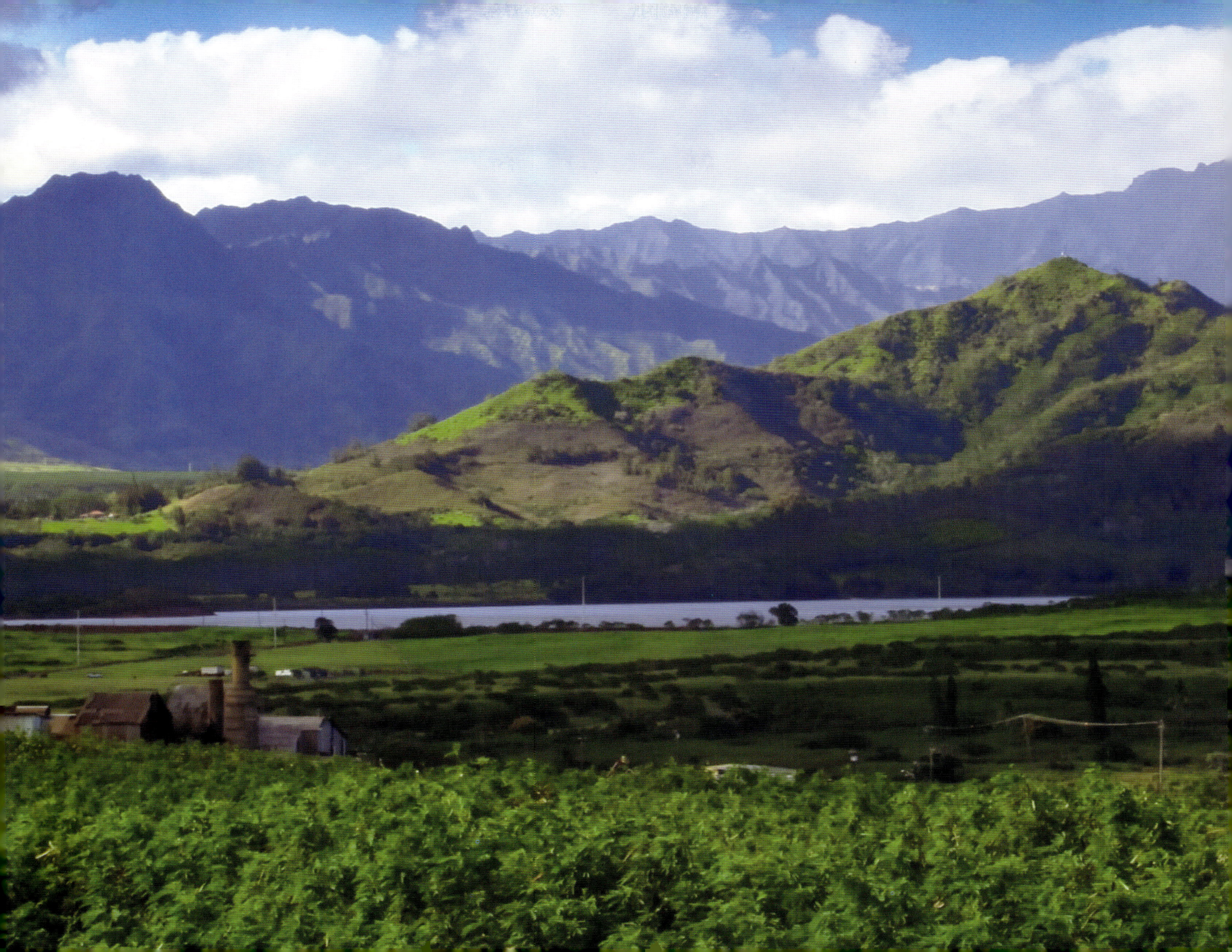

conflict of interest from the Grove Farm board. It was arranged that other members of the firm Case Bigelow & Lombardi would do Grove Farm's work while the acquisition was in discussions.

The Cases were clear that they did not want an unfriendly negotiation.

"We wanted to be sure we were invited in," Steve Case said.

And they were. Klebahn invited Steve Case to submit an offer, and he did so through ALPS Investment LLC, which was owned by his personal revocable living trust. The offer was $152 per share for the outstanding 171,122 shares, with an ALPS subsidiary to merge with Grove Farm and Grove Farm to be the surviving entity. It worked out to about $26 million in cash, with Case to assume the $62 million in debt. It put the value of the acquisition at $88 million.

Steve Case said that as AOL soared in value during the late 1990s, he began selling off chunks of shares in order to diversify his financial situation. So he had significant cash available for investments. He had already invested in the Islands with the purchase of Harry Weinberg's forty percent stake in Maui Land & Pine.

"When Grove Farm came around, my dad was interested. When the opportunity came up, I thought it would be a good investment. Ultimately, I didn't have time to do a lot of diligence. There was a time constraint," Steve Case said. He sent his investment manager, John Agee, to study the company and the land, and on his positive recommendation, Case made an offer that was higher than the Honu Group's highest offer.

Case's offer was compelling, said Donn Carswell, an engineer who had helped build the Kuʻia-Waitā water tunnel as a Grove Farm employee. He was now a member of the Grove Farm board and served as a member of the board committee reviewing offers. "We had a lot of people who came and kicked the tires, but when push came to shove, most of them couldn't perform, financially," Carswell said.

A stockholders meeting was held at the Carriage House at Kilohana, once the home of a Grove Farm manager Gaylord Parke Wilcox. Grove Farm's shareholders voted 98.9 percent in favor of accepting the Case offer. Carswell said the board faced a hard deadline to make a decision. Case's proposal was a fair offer, he said.

Interestingly, the decision by the vast majority of shareholders to sell the company to Steve Case was built on some of the same foundations that caused George N. Wilcox nearly eighty years earlier to distribute shares to his family members—with the majority of shares voted in trust by family members who had actually been raised on Grove Farm.

His goal was to see that his vision and his company would be carried forward, and not chopped up and sold off. Several people close to the sale said they recognized that Grove Farm might have been able to survive, albeit as a much smaller company, if it had sold off large chunks of its land and used the proceeds to pay down debt.

Ultimately, several family members said they voted to sell it whole to Steve Case, comfortable that he had the resources to keep the company together.

"What we envisioned when we sold it to the Case family was that the traditions would carry on," said David Pratt.

Once the deal was done, minority shareholders filed legal complaints that would continue through hearings and appeals until as late as 2010. The courts ultimately confirmed the sale of Grove Farm to Steve Case.

And now Grove Farm, for the first time since George Norton Wilcox transferred his interests to family members, was once again held entirely by a single individual.

Dan Case said his motives in inviting his son to bid for Grove Farm were two. He had a personal emotional attachment to the land, having grown

Above: *Steve Case: The overarching message is, "Let's do what's right."*

"I worked seven days a week for years."

Michiye Funaku, who brought Grove Farm into the computer age, was born eighty-three years ago on a Kona coffee farm, but moved to Kaua'i as a child during the depression, when her father took a position with Grove Farm. They lived in company housing at Aakukui.

Her dad had arrived in Hawai'i from Japan and found work as an Olokele Sugar Company ditch man—managing the plantation's complex upland irrigation system. At the time, he told his daughter, he and another ditch man, who was Chinese, lived in a cave in the mountains. Later he worked for Grove Farm, moved to Kona to work in coffee and returned to take a job at Grove Farm as a track man, laying railroad track. Her mother arrived in the Islands as a picture bride from Japan, never having met the man she would marry.

As a young girl, Michiye helped cook, wait tables and sometimes babysit at the home of then-company-president Gaylord P. Wilcox. Her mother, who was a servant in the Wilcox house, wanted better for her daughter. "She wanted me to concentrate on school and not end up working in that house," she said.

Funaku was taught bookkeeping by Marie Case, the second wife of Steve Case's grandfather, Hib Case. Young Michiye was working as a temporary postal clerk at Puhi Store when Grove Farm office manager Fred Lawrence approached her. "He urged me to apply at Grove Farm," Funaku said.

Funaku thought twice. "I was making good money at the post office—federal wages." But in August 1950, Funaku took a job at the Grove Farm office in Puhi, using a clumsy early accounting machine to post employee hours.

"Pretty soon I was running a huge payroll machine that printed out checks, " she recalled, "and then I was promoted to timekeeper. I went to Honolulu about 1955 for six weeks for IBM training in board wiring—in those days programming was done through wiring. Later we punched programs into big cards, then smaller cards." Finally she programmed directly via the keyboard on a Hewlett-Packard machine.

"Nobody else was trained on that equipment," she said. "I worked seven days a week for years. I had my own covered parking spot next to (company president) David Pratt's."

Funaku lived in Kaipu Camp, then in Puhi Camp, before getting married and buying homes successively in Wailua Houselots, then Grove Farm subdivisions in Pua Loke and finally Ulu Mahi. Her husband, Stanley, worked at Hawaiian Canneries, at the Hawaiian Sugar Planters Association and at a chemical company before he retired.

Michiye Fujimoto Funaku

up here when his father was the Grove Farm bookkeeper and later chief financial officer and corporate treasurer. And it seemed like a way to tie son Steve to Hawai'i, as he now lived far away on the East Coast and seemed likely to stay there.

For Steve Case, the purchase was an investment in a land-rich company that looked like it could increase in value given enough time. Case, wrapped up in running AOL, sent a financial representative to tour the Grove Farm property and to look at the books. The recommendation was positive.

"It really was viewing it as kind of a long-term investment, from a financial perspective, mostly in the context of diversification—deploying some capital and owning land that over time we would hope would go up in value. And it seemed like a reasonable price," Steve Case said.

And what about running the company while waiting for the value to rise?

"I figured my dad and the management team would figure out what to do with it," Steve Case said. "I was super busy at the time still running AOL, and I wouldn't have bought it if he hadn't been ready to step in to help run the company."

Dan Case said his own proposal was to turn over management to someone very familiar with the land and the company, and someone who had his own family connection to Grove Farm. "I told him when he bought it, I would be chairman, and I would try to hire David Pratt."

Pratt's ties to Grove Farm were deep. His grandfather, E.H.W. Broadbent, had spent thirty years in the early 1900s as G.N. Wilcox's plantation manager at Grove Farm. Pratt's father, Dudley Pratt Sr., had been Grove Farm's corporate attorney. Pratt himself had spent nearly two decades as Grove Farm's president.

And Pratt had another family connection. His first wife, Debbie, was the daughter of Wilcox heir and former Grove Farm president Sam Wilcox. Thus, Pratt's sons, Sam and Bill, are Wilcox descendants.

It is a different connection from the Case family's but in some ways eerily familiar.

Both the Case and the Pratt families have connections to Grove Farm that span multiple generations.

David Pratt's grandfather and Steve Case's grandfather worked side by side at Grove Farm.

David Pratt's father and Steve Case's father were law partners and were both corporate attorneys for Grove Farm.

And David Pratt was president of Grove Farm when Steve Case first bought it. And Pratt currently serves on the board with Steve Case's father.

By the time Steve Case bought Grove Farm, the plantation was a shadow of its former self. Once an aggressive player in the Hawaiian sugar industry, with thousands of acres in crop, hundreds of workers and an advanced sugar mill, it was now a company near bankruptcy with just eight employees.

How to proceed? It was clear from the beginning that Steve Case did not have a grand scheme for the future of Grove Farm. He bought it because his advisers said it seemed like a solid land deal, and because of his father's personal attachment to the land.

Also, he bought it because he was actively looking for ways to diversify his wealth, which was largely tied to AOL, the Internet company he ran. Farm land in Hawai'i seemed about as diversified as you could get from the high-tech online world.

His father, Dan Case, who had been involved with Grove Farm for decades, felt the company had had a sound master plan that had been undercut by an economic downturn—a downturn fueled by both the Gulf War and Hurricane Iniki. With Steve Case's purchase and his financial stability putting the company back on sound financial ground, it seemed reasonable to return to that master plan, Dan Case said.

Case turned to Pratt, who had left during some of the company's darkest days. Case recalls that it took about a month to convince him to return to Grove Farm, but Pratt himself said he wasn't so hard to sell. "I wanted them to succeed," Pratt said.

"Once David took over, I was a non-executive chairman, and Steve didn't interfere at all. The master plan that David had gotten back then was good, and we are still working off that master plan today."

That is not to say that Steve Case wasn't involved and engaged. He remains an active player in the top-level decisions for Grove Farm and he participates in most board of directors meetings, either in person or electronically.

"Steve brings tremendous value. He's aware of new innovations and concepts, and we are probably much more innovative because of him," said Warren Haruki, who succeeded Pratt as president. "His overarching message is, 'Let's do what's right.'

"We're fortunate in having a solid entrepreneur interested in a double bottom line and sometimes a triple bottom line. And that is a very good thing for the island."

As soon as Case took ownership and Pratt

"In the plantation days, agriculture really was the economy. Now it's more difficult to focus on ag."

Above: Warren Haruki: *"Collaboration is a key to success."*

resumed the helm, there was plenty of work to do. One of the first significant actions after the purchase of the company was a multi-million-dollar debt deal. Grove Farm owed close to $62 million in loans from First Hawaiian Bank and Bank of Hawai'i. Shortly after the Case purchase of the company, First Hawaiian president Walter Dods contacted Pratt.

"Walter Dods called and offered Grove Farm a $10 million discount on its debt to clean up its books, if we could finish the deal before the end of the year," Dan Case said. Steve Case took the deal, although instead of paying it off, Steve bought the loan.

During a Christmas visit shortly after the Grove Farm purchase, Steve Case visited and noticed that most of neighboring Lihue Plantation was for sale. Sections of the plantation near Hanamā'ulu and Kealia had already been sold off. But Case noticed that the company's residential projects in the Līhu'e area could end up being competition for Grove Farm's own developments.

Dan Case tells the story, "Steve came down for Christmas. He looked at some Līhu'e housing projects and said, 'We'll be competing with them. Why don't we buy it?' We offered to buy the remaining portion of the Lihue Plantation, got it appraised, and worried about the environmental issues around Lihue Mill and one other site."

Negotiations for the nearly 18,000 acres bounced between $20 million and $26 million. Eventually, Steve bought most of the land, but not the mill, for roughly $25 million, his father said. That gave him close to 40,000 acres on the island—all of the original Grove Farm land, plus the original Koloa Plantation land, plus much of the Lihue Plantation land.

Despite this and other indications of Grove Farm's new financial strength under Steve Case's ownership, the two major banks were still unwilling to loan money to Grove Farm.

Dan Case jokes that he wasn't entirely surprised, since even he did not have a clear idea of what Steve's net worth might be.

"I had never known the extent of Steve's wealth," Dan Case said. (*Forbes* in June 2014 estimated it at $1.3 billion.)

When the company wanted to build a surface water treatment facility to support its development plans, the two big Hawai'i banks would not finance it. Grove Farm turned to smaller Central Pacific Bank, which loaned the money. According to Dan Case, Central Pacific Bank's willingness to take on Grove Farm financing helped convince First Hawaiian and Bank of Hawai'i that the company was once again a good risk. "The CPB loan turned the corner for us," he said.

A year or so after the purchase of Grove Farm, Steve Case asked the company's board why the company was running a shopping center, and whether they should sell. "It didn't seem like a core function for Grove Farm," Dan Case said.

Warren Haruki expanded: "The shopping center was not a strategic fit, and it (the sale of the center) was a vehicle to reduce debt. We sold it for $63 million to the Alaska Permanent Fund. We used some of that money to start the Grove Farm Foundation. We put $250,000 a year into the Foundation, and it's now near $3 million with contributions and appreciation."

"It cleared the books of some debt and provided some working capital," Dan Case said.

With the shopping center sold off, Grove Farm built out the remaining portion of the Puakea Golf Course, which had been stopped at ten holes during the troubles of the 1990s. It was brought to eighteen holes. House lots on the golf course and nearby were marketed, as were commercial lots.

"We're a land company, and we're trying to branch out in as many areas as we can," Dan Case said.

Steve Case responds with a similar message, but in more detail.

"In the plantation days, agriculture really was the economy. At the peak of the ag revolution, ninety-eight percent of the jobs in America were in ag, and now it's two percent. Now it is more difficult to focus on ag. We are recognizing that businesses have to reinvent themselves. Grove Farm has tried to do that," he said.

"We are trying to find the businesses that can work, can provide vitality to the community while continuing stewardship responsibly. What we do with the land impacts what happens in the community. Being good stewards to the land is the driver.

"We are looking for a creative way of developing land. We've committed half the land to important agricultural use. We're committed to working with partners, as we're not the experts on everything," Steve Case said.

As George N. Wilcox formed partnerships with neighboring plantations, with shipping interests, with irrigation clients and others, the modern Grove Farm also recognizes the value of working with others.

"Collaboration is a key to success. You cannot have a self-driven agenda," Haruki said.

Another feature of the modern Grove Farm that is similar to that of early Grove Farm is the long view. One of the things that troubled Grove Farm during its middle years was the demand to deliver regular dividends to shareholders.

Whether it was George Wilcox or Steve Case, having a single owner with strong financial resources allowed the company to forgo near-term performance for a more distant objective.

"It's a different approach, and a patient approach. Grove Farm has a single owner and a longer term view," Steve Case said.

Grove Farm's nēnē goose habitat is located on the shores of the Kapaia Reservoir—the open space across from the surface water treatment plant, between the ironwood grove at center and the small cove at right. In the company's partnership with the State Division of Forestry and Wildlife, goslings are relocated from the Kaua'i Lagoons resort area, where they are at risk from collisions with aircraft at Lihue Airport.

Chapter 7
The Initiatives

"How to use the land responsibly. How to create more jobs and homes. These things in any community are interconnected and are particularly connected on an island. Everybody has to work together in a collaborative way. We are trying to find the businesses that can work, can provide vitality to the community while continuing stewardship responsibly." —Steve Case

"We're a land company, and we're trying to branch out in as many ways as we can." —Dan Case

Steve Case had been to Kaua'i often as a child, but bought Grove Farm without having been back in many years. He relied for advice on his investment manager John Agee, who flew to the island to tour the plantation, and his father, Dan Case, both of whom recommended the purchase of the company.

But when Case first visited the island after buying Grove Farm, it was not what he remembered and his reaction was disappointment.

He had remembered a vibrant countryside, rich in green irrigated sugar cane, with a bustling agricultural workforce. What he found was a weedy landscape, much of it no longer in agricultural use. As the new owner of the property, his goal, he said, became to find a way to use his investment to help return Grove Farm to health and also to help the community.

"We are trying to turn the ag land into something that was a productive use. We thought that was one good thing. And an energy community…renewables are something I've been interested in. There are pluses and minuses of being a small island with a small population. Kaua'i could be the first energy self-sufficient community in the country. It seemed like there was an opportunity to do that," Case said.

He sought a triple bottom line for the company—a term sometimes rendered as people-planet-profit. The company needed to support the community, to sustain the environment and to make economic sense.

There was a housing component in Grove Farm's existing plans and that would continue.

And the company has always engaged in innovation when it came to water. Wilcox developed some of the most challenging irrigation systems in all Hawai'i, bringing water to fields other farmers couldn't figure out how to irrigate. Case's Grove Farm built the first surface water treatment facility of its kind on Kaua'i.

Case has some of the same instincts as George Norton Wilcox when it comes to charitable endeavors. Sometimes Wilcox gave people cash, but

Top and Right: *The Pikake subdivision, one of Grove Farm's newest, includes 180 lots on the Puakea Golf Course, with views of the Hā'upu Range.*
Above: *The company commissioned Hawai'i artist Leah Kilpatrick-Rigg to create a series of native plant mosaics on the Pikake wall along Nuhou Street.*

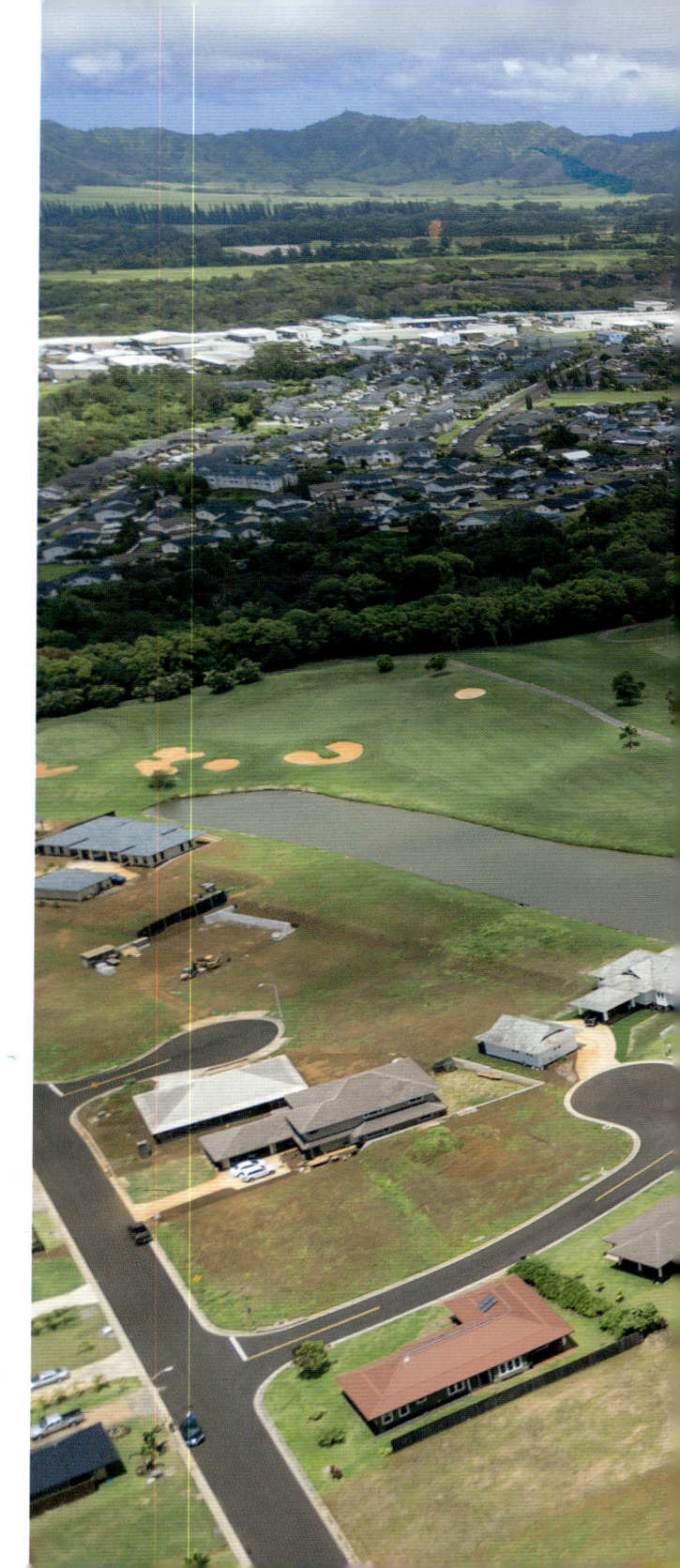

100   GROVE FARM, KAUA'I: 150 Years of Stewardship and Innovation

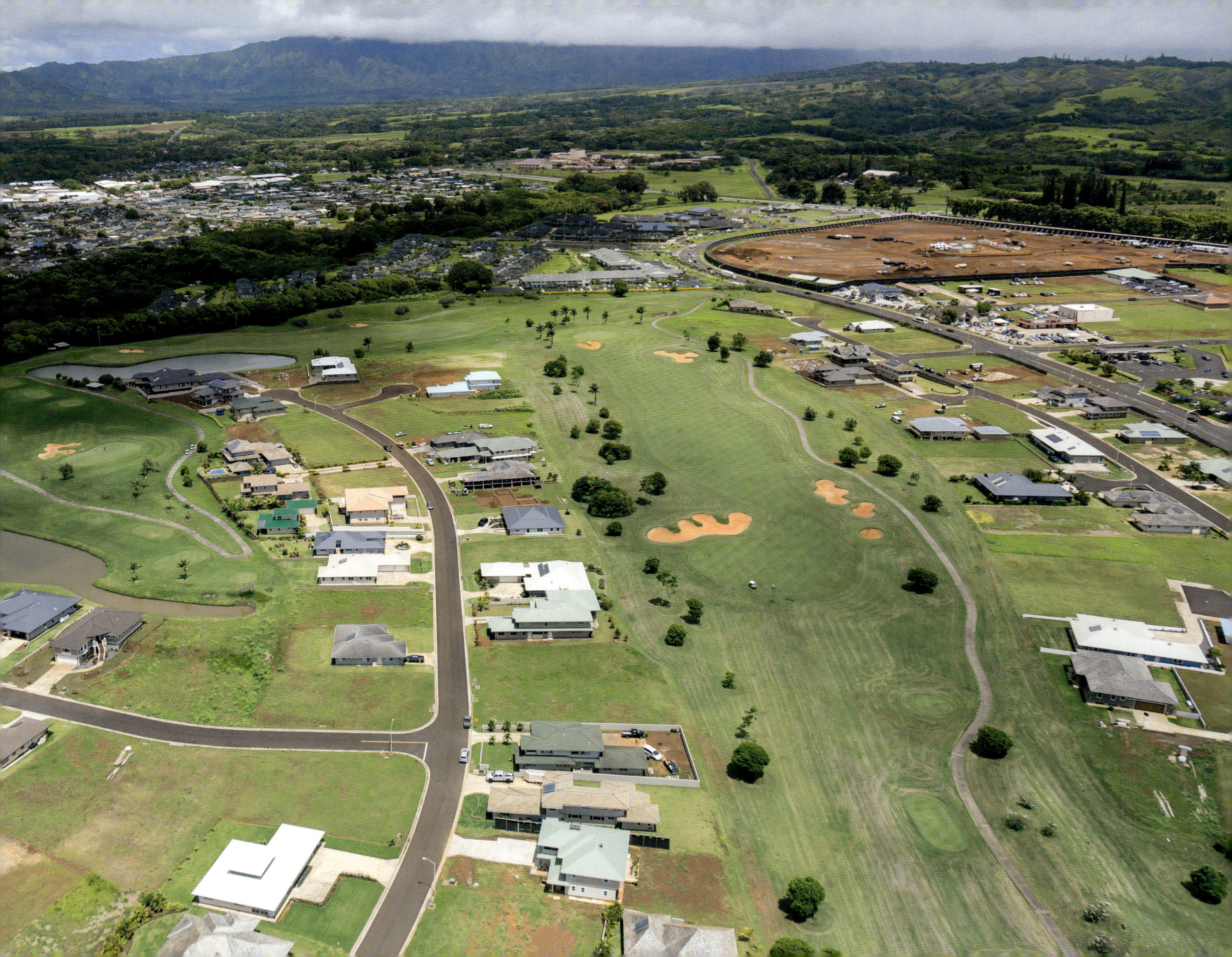

often, he tried to help them take care of themselves. One of his drivers recalls Wilcox gave a fishing net to a needy Hawaiian man with a large family. Under Case, Grove Farm provided farmland for victims of human trafficking through the Pacific Gateway Center program.

Case's initial goals were unspecific references to agriculture and energy. He needed a much more focused approach and he recognized that. "I'm not sure exactly what the right path forward is, so trying different things became a key focus."

His father's recommendation had been to ask David Pratt, the former company president, to come back and try to get the company moving again. There was an existing master plan, whose development Pratt had overseen, and it had been sidelined by an economic crisis. Dan Case decided to see if that plan could still work. And Pratt's second term at the helm indeed brought stability to the company. The company trimmed non-core functions, built on initiatives that were appropriate to continue and expanded into new areas that seemed to make sense.

"We sold the shopping center. We had subdivisions in progress and we restarted those. We continued planning for new subdivisions. We did leasing. We sold vacant lots in Village West," Pratt said.

One of the company's oldest missions has been to provide housing for local residents. In the earliest days, George Wilcox built plantation camps to house his employees. Later, the company built subdivisions that its workers could own. The new Grove Farm continued its focus on residential development with the island's residents in mind. There is evidence that plan is succeeding. Some ninety-five percent of the lots in its Pikake subdivision, as an example, sold to Kaua'i residents.

The company sold a large commercial parcel to The Home Depot, which opened in October 2003. Another big lot went to Costco, which opened in October 2006. Additional developable property has been sold to organizations like Property Development Centers, which has developed the Hōkūlei Village shopping complex.

Grove Farm's 150-year-old commitment to education has continued. George Norton Wilcox helped found Malumalu School in the Līhu'e area, and was a major supporter of Mid-Pacific Institute and Punahou School on O'ahu. Sam Wilcox donated 200 acres of Grove Farm Land to provide a campus for Kaua'i Community College. Case in 2006 donated 8.45 acres of land to Island School through his Lihue Land Co. The company set up the Grove Farm Foundation on the sale of the Lihue Shopping Center, funding it at a rate of $250,000 annually. Among its missions is scholarships for

---

Left: Where Grove Farm cane once grew, the Puako subdivision in Līhu'e is comprised of 105 lots, most of which have been built on by local residents.
Right: Grove Farm's Puhi industrial subdivision (foreground) lies adjacent to the company's several residential projects makai of the project.

Kaua'i students. It currently provides four-year scholarships to students from the island's three public high schools.

And there has been a great deal more. Here are some of the major initiatives that Grove Farm has undertaken during the Case years.

Environmental Initiatives

Grove Farm is raising *nēnē*—the Hawaiian state bird. It is growing and outplanting *maile*. And it is re-establishing native species on the slopes of Kilohana Crater below the Iliahi Estate.

Its restoration is in many ways similar to those of George Norton Wilcox a century and a half ago, but in other ways quite different. Wilcox and some of his successors in running the plantation despaired of the loss of native forest habitat.

There are reports in the files of Grove Farm Homestead Museum about a worm that was wiping out the kukui forests in which Grove Farm had initially been established. Early Grove Farm executives recall hiking the slopes of Kilohana Crater and worrying about falling into the holes left by ancient rotting giant koa trees.

Wilcox, as is described elsewhere in this book, was a reforester of some note. He collected trees from around the world and tried them out on his lands. Sometimes they appeared successful—he extolled the wood quality of Norfolk pines. Sometimes there were problems with specific trees—he complained that the roots of ironwood competed with his sugar cane. But he was a tree planter as well as a food crop planter his whole life. Modern Grove Farm is working extensively with partners to grow food crops as well—dairy cattle, beef cattle, grains, taro, papaya, sweet potato, corn, ginger and other vegetables. Like Wilcox, modern Grove Farm also uses its land to grow trees—nearly 600 acres of them.

In its restoration work, modern Grove Farm is outplanting some of the native landscape whose decline Wilcox despaired of.

In one project, Grove Farm personnel collected seeds from the prized native *lei* plant maile (*Alyxia oliviformis*) and sprouted seedlings in a small greenhouse. The small-leafed maile, *maile-lau-li'i*, is the signature lei of Kaua'i, often entwined with the anise-scented fruits of the *mokihana* shrub. Maile is often overharvested by lei-making islanders, and Grove Farm's goal in collecting seeds and sprouting them was to restore the natural stock of the scented vine on Grove Farm land.

The maile seedlings have been replanted in the wild on Grove Farm land, generally in the 'Ili'ili'ula area. They also have been planted out by students and volunteers in a forest restoration effort on the eastern slope of Kilohana Crater, the Grove Farm Ecological Restoration Project. Collaborators included the State Department of Land and Natural Resources staff, the Kaua'i Invasive Species Committee and the University of Hawai'i at Mānoa Botany Department, as well as the National Tropical Botanical Garden.

There, maile joins some 2,500 other native plants of several species, including the native

---

Left: Kaua'i Community College's Puhi campus lies on 200 acres donated to the University of Hawai'i by Grove Farm when Sam Wilcox was the company's president.
Right: Island School's Puhi campus, started on land donated by Amfac, was subsequently expanded with Grove Farm's donation of an eight-acre adjacent parcel. The private school holds classes from preschool to grade 12.

As Grove Farm moved from sugar to development, its key projects grew around the Kukui Grove Center (top center), including Kmart below it, Costco at left center, The Home Depot above that and beyond, the Hōkūlei Village shopping center, under development and still in the bare-dirt stage.

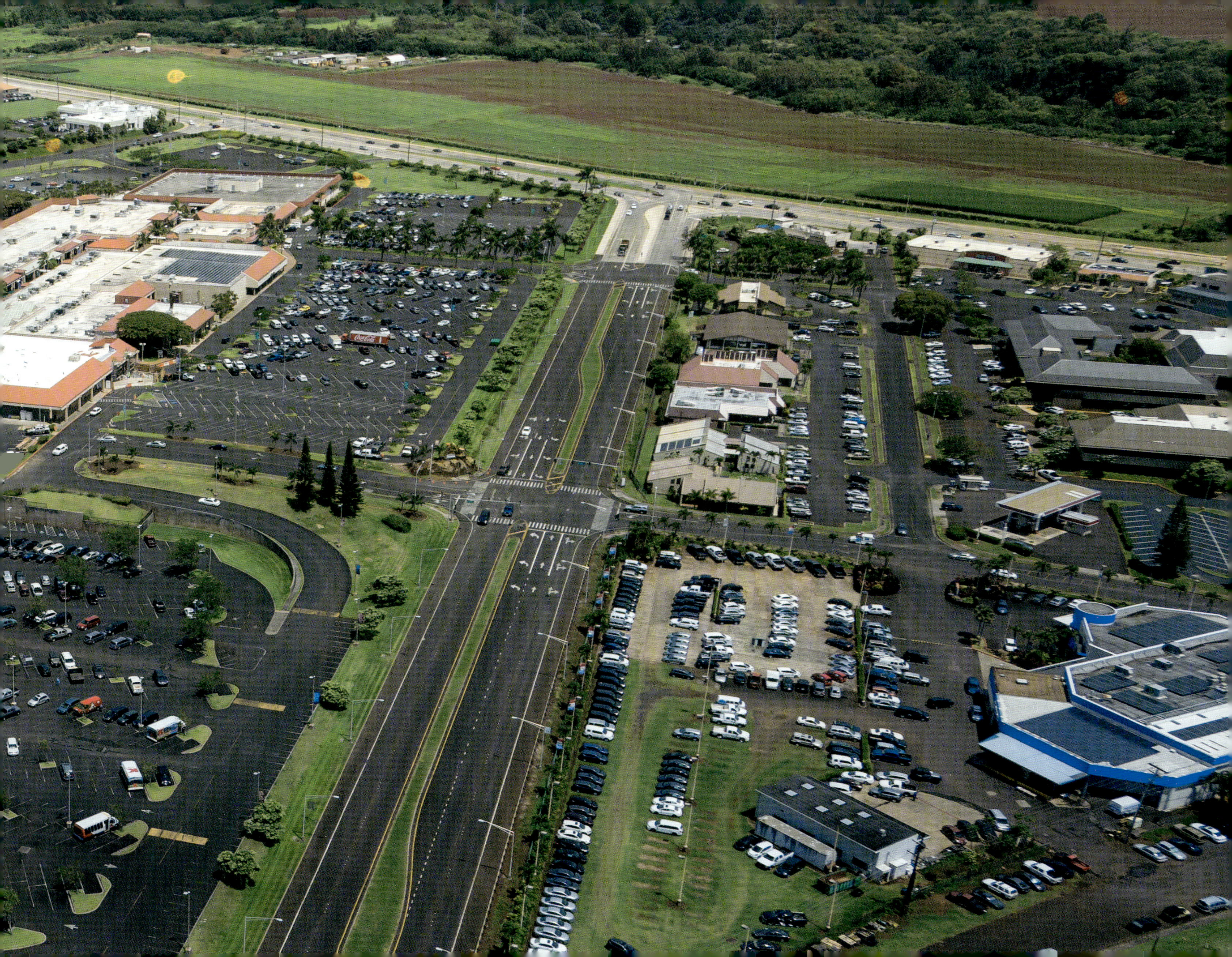

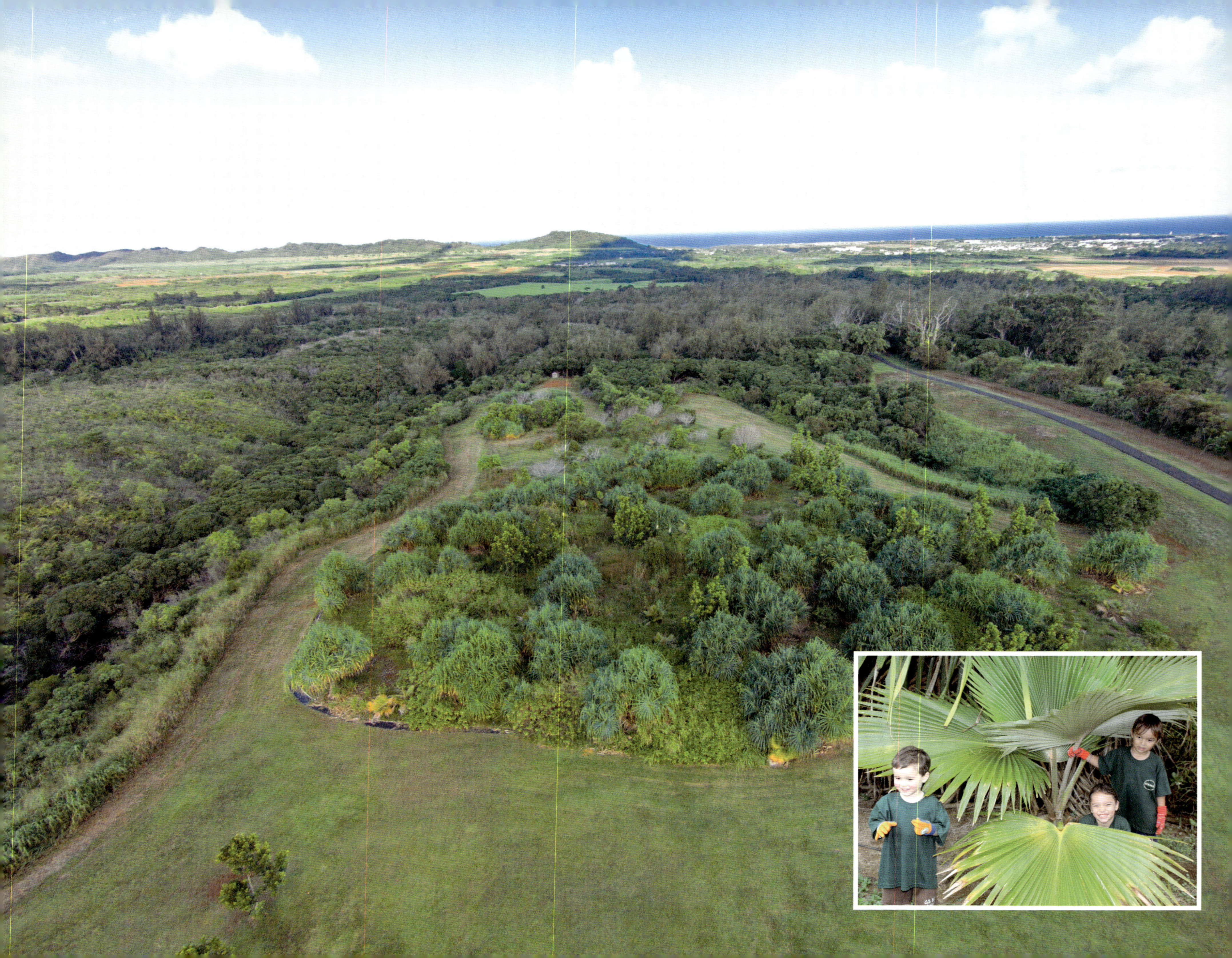

George N. Wilcox's Plantings

Replanting native plants is nothing new at Grove Farm. Founder G.N. Wilcox was an inveterate planter, not only of food crops, but of timber plants and curiosities. Some of his thoughts on the subject:

"Frank Judd...brought a box of seeds from Australia and somehow it got left out by my cottage for years—till all the seeds had grown. That's where the two *kawi* ("kauri") pines came from. For a long time I had no idea what they were. Then somebody came along who knew...

"Those tall palms by the office, Chinese fan palms...have been growing there a long time too. A German gave me the seed, the man who lived where the Pacific Club is now, or just below. Riemenschneider his name was...he was very fond of palms.

"If I were to live another hundred years I would plant Norfolk pines. We think they are a valuable tree for posts and piles... We used some of those trees for fence posts along the new Kilohana road where it went through those upper cane fields.

"The first ironwood seeds I got was when W.O. Smith was sheriff and he planted some at the old courthouse...we planted all along the road up to Halehaka...but the roots got into the cane field and they had to come out.

"The durian tree? That came from Kalakaua's trip around the world. Charlie Judd and W.N. Armstrong went along with him and from several places they sent back young trees. Jaeger had charge of the plants when they arrived in Honolulu. And he sent them out to different people all over the Islands. I had a durian and a mangosteen, the purple Malay mangosteen.

"Kahele Laweleka (mail carrier), on his way once a week to take letters to Hanalei, had a mulberry switch in his hand. I took it away from him and planted it. They grow easily from slip, you know, like hau and make quite a big trunk as a tree, big around as your arm.

"Ti leaf is a valuable plant, the leaf for cooking and now often as an ornamental plant, and we boys used to have the root for chewing. Of course, they make okolehao from it, but not so much in those days. I think it was forbidden by law."

---

loulu palms *Pritchardia viscosa* and *Pritchardia hardyi*, *mamaki* trees, *palapalai* ferns, *'ōhi'a*, the exceedly rare *Polyscias racemosa* (formerly known as *Munroidendron racemosum*), a couple of species of native hibiscus, *'alahe'e*, *kamani*, *hala* and many more.

In addition to planting out the native species, Boy Scouts, Girl Scouts, elementary and middle school students and others conducted scientific experiments on growth and survivorship of the plants, and participated in sustainability awareness activities.

Grove Farm has worked with the State Division of Forestry and Wildlife to create dedicated habitat for nēnē, the Hawaiian goose. The birds were moved from areas next to Lihue Airport, where both the birds themselves and aircraft were in danger from the potential of birds being drawn into jet engines.

The nēnē habitat is on the shores of the Kapaia Reservoir, and is fenced to keep the Hawaiian state bird safe from predators like dogs and feral pigs.

"Our objective is to create a safe habitat where nēnē geese can feed, nest and flourish. Because nēnē have been known to 'imprint' on an area and return to use these areas as nesting sites, it is our hope that the goslings will return to this safe area. Already, some nēnē from previous releases have been observed returning to the area. The Grove Farm's Nēnē Goose Habitat Initiative has provided a safe breeding zone for our state bird," said Grove Farm vice president Marissa Sandblom.

Hawaii Dairy Farms

Beef cattle and milk cows have been part of Grove Farm since the beginning. George N. Wilcox ran cattle on some of his non-sugar lands, and sometimes ran cattle on cane lands between crops when he was letting the land lie fallow. Milk from cows was part of the service that plantations provided to their employees on most plantations.

"One of my first memories of Grove Farm was bringing over milk in here to the kitchen in the morning, to get our supply of milk, which the cowboys obtained from a few fresh animals," said William P. Alexander, who would manage the plantation in the mid-1900s.

Some plantations sold milk outside their own

Left: Students, scouts and other volunteers have helped plant and manage several acres of land being reforested in native species. This site lies just below the Iliahi house on the slope of Kilohana Crater, where a wide range of native and Polynesian introduced species have been planted. The dominant species in the circle at center right is the pandanus, or hala tree.
Inset: Island youth among native plants at Iliahi.

workforce, but at Grove Farm the homestead dairy operations never went commercial.

"We would bring in the cows with the fresh calves into the backyard and in the adjoining pasture, we always had about twenty cows being milked," said Gaylord P. Wilcox.

Grove Farm had not planned a commercial dairy within its operations until Pierre and Pam Omidyar's Ulupono Initiative brought forth its proposal to lease land from Grove Farm for a state-of-the-art milk production operation.

There had been some planning for resorts by Grove Farm along its coastline from Poʻipū to Māhāʻulepū, but they have faced significant community opposition, and under Steve Case, any plans along those lines seemed to be fading. "I don't ever see the resort we planned (in Māhāʻulepū) coming to pass. That's one reason for the dairy," Dan Case said.

Grove Farm was committed to farming locally generated agricultural crops, and that seemed a good fit with Ulupono, which describes itself as "a for-profit impact investment firm focusing on sustaining Hawaiʻi through investments that produce more local food, increase clean, renewable energy and reduce waste."

Ulupono and Grove Farm discussed various areas on Grove Farm land and settled on the Māhāʻulepū Valley, a broad, flat plain cradled against the southern face of the Hāʻupu Range. The land was previously in sugar cane and parts of it have been growing diversified crops like taro.

In 2013, Ulupono launched its $17.5 million program to establish a grass-fed dairy on 582 acres of Māhāʻulepū Valley land. Its goal was to produce fresh local milk for sale in school lunch programs and for the general public at affordable prices.

Ulupono's Hawaii Dairy Farms partnered with Dairy Solutionz (NZ) Ltd., the life sciences venture capital firm Finistere Ventures LLC and Atlantic Dairy Consulting LLC, for a sustainable dairying operation using rotationally grazed pastures. In addition to direct jobs, it would partner with local ranchers to support cattle ranching island wide.

Hawaiʻi BioEnergy

"Why can't Kauaʻi be energy independent? We started with that question. That was the genesis of our involvement in Hawaiʻi BioEnergy," said Grove Farm president Warren Haruki.

The concept for Hawaiʻi BioEnergy came from the head of another company in which Steve Case is heavily invested, Maui Land & Pine. The company's then-president David Cole had proposed a collaboration of investment capital firms and major landowners in the Islands to research and develop new renewable energy sources.

In 2006, Hawaiʻi BioEnergy, LLC was formed by three of Hawaiʻi's largest landowners–Grove Farm, Maui Land & Pineapple Company and Kamehameha Schools, along with Finistere Ventures LLC, Vinod Khosla's venture capital firm Khosla Ventures and Pierre Omidyar's investment firm, ʻOhana Holdings, LLC.

"It's got a real future, not only will it lead to locally-sourced electricity, but it will use land that is otherwise pretty much unusable," said Dan Case.

One of the earliest initiatives involving Grove Farm was an innovative algae farming project that aimed to make affordable fuel from the natural oils in certain varieties of algae. Partners SAIC (Science Applications International Corporation) and General Atomics worked under a grant from the Defense Advanced Research Projects Agency. Their goal was to conduct the basic research that would lead to the ability to efficiently produce military jet fuel (JP-8) from oil-rich crops produced by agriculture or aquaculture.

The project was built next to electric company Kauaʻi Island Utility Cooperative's Kapaia power plant so that it could use the carbon-dioxide-rich power plant exhaust to feed the algae. By the time the project wrapped up in 2012, according to Joel Matsunaga, Hawaiʻi BioEnergy chief operating officer, it had proven the concept.

Once the research program's funding ended, the algae ponds lay fallow for a little more than a year, and then Hawaiʻi BioEnergy and Grove Farm launched a new algae venture in cooperation with Texas A&M University and Global Algae Innovations. The partners are using eight acres of wet ponds on about thirty-three acres of former sugar cane land to conduct more work toward making liquid fuel from algae, but also to study other algae products, such as nutrient-rich supplements for humans and animal feed.

In another project, Hawaiʻi BioEnergy is working to partner with companies that have the technology to convert woody biomass into liquid fuels, and hopes to develop projects that will create liquid fuels under contract for the Hawaiian Electric utilities. Matsunaga said the system can use trees and other woody crops grown on the Hawaiʻi BioEnergy partner lands.

Hawaiʻi BioEnergy is also looking at a range of other projects, such as producing biogas from a variety of grown products for use as utility or transportation fuel.

Left and Opposite: *Sales of produce at a Grove Farm fruit stand in Kōloa-Poʻipū help support farmers growing crops on company acreage.*

THE INITIATIVES 109

Grove Farm's Wailani project establishes a new urban center along both sides of Ahukini Road from Walmart (foreground) to Lihue Airport, visible in the distance. It will include residential, commercial, industrial, school, park and other facilities for local residents.

"A life of resilience and resourcefulness"

Stanley Viluan, 74, was born in Waimea and grew up in Spanish Camp in Kekaha, and then Japanese Camp near Kekaha Mill. As a boy he worked summers as a field hand with Kekaha Sugar Company, and planted pineapple at Makaha Ridge for sale to Kauai Pine. He joined contractor Kentron, building launching pads at the Pacific Missile Range Facility's Sandia rocket launching facility. Eventually, Kentron lost the contract and Viluan was out of work.

When he applied at Grove Farm, he wasn't sure they really wanted him since they offered him what he considered the toughest job on the plantation—a fertilizer applicator. He took that job, and later moved to drilling water wells and then to Grove Farm's rock crushing operations.

He was among the first workers to move to the new site when Grove Farm expanded its Halfway Bridge blue rock operation to the crushed limestone plant at Māhāʻulepu. They made sand, crushed limestone rock and agricultural lime. "We didn't waste anything."

"Crusher workers had to be flexible. We were just a handful. We did sales, quarrying, demolition. Eventually we set up a portable crushing plant that we moved around, to Kapaia, Kekaha, Kīlauea. Sometimes we crushed river rock or rock that came up in cane farming.

"We sold rock to the state and county for roads. We provided rock for the airport runway. We made sand so contractors could make concrete."

Since crusher work involved blasting, meaning he had experience with explosives, Viluan also worked on the construction of the 12,000-foot Kūʻia-Waitā water tunnel.

"I lost my hearing in there. After we drilled the holes, the powder man would go in. We would back off, but we were still in the tunnel when the blast went. It would blow off your hat, and blow your lunch right out of your hands," Viluan said.

Viluan was a hunter, fisherman and a diver. He remembers in the days before nylon line, net fishermen would boil their linen nets in water and ironwood bark to strengthen them. That was cheaper than buying pre-treated netting from Japan. For diving, they would make their own spearfishing equipment, buying spring steel from a local metalworker.

Hunting, fishing, gathering and growing food and making the necessary tools—life on the plantations required resilience and resourcefulness.

Stanley Viluan

Grove Farm is also involved in other energy projects, including a sixty-seven-acre photovoltaic array site leased to the Kaua'i Island Utility Cooperative (KIUC) near Koloa Mill. At the completion of construction this year, the twelve-megawatt solar farm was the largest photovoltaic facility in the state.

Small-Scale Agriculture

Throughout its long history, Grove Farm has been in the diversified agriculture business, either through growing crops like pineapple, ti, macadamia nuts and lychee itself, or by leasing land for small cattle operations and crops like flowers, papaya and Hawaiian pia or arrowroot.

The company continues in its current ownership to investigate and support opportunities for its thousands of acres of agricultural lands. One option under consideration is greenhouse aquaponics at the Koloa Mill site. Another is the potential of a breadfruit farm in cooperation with the National Tropical Botanical Garden's Breadfruit Institute.

Not far from the mill, in Māhā'ulepū Valley, the company has leased fifty acres for taro cultivation to two local farmers.

"We feel there are lots more small crop applications," Haruki said.

At this writing, Grove Farm had 3,298 acres in food and flower production, 6,458 acres in cattle ranching, 582 acres in dairy, 537 acres in tree crops, thirty-three acres in its algae farm and sixty-seven acres leased for the photovoltaic array operated by KIUC.

Above: Grove Farm, Solar City and the Kaua'i Island Utility Cooperative worked together to develop a solar photovoltaic system on sixty-seven acres just below the Waitā Reservoir. At the time of its dedication in 2014, the twelve-megawatt solar array was by far the largest in the state.
Right: The old Koloa Mill stands at upper left of the solar panels—a dramatic juxtaposition of old and new technology.

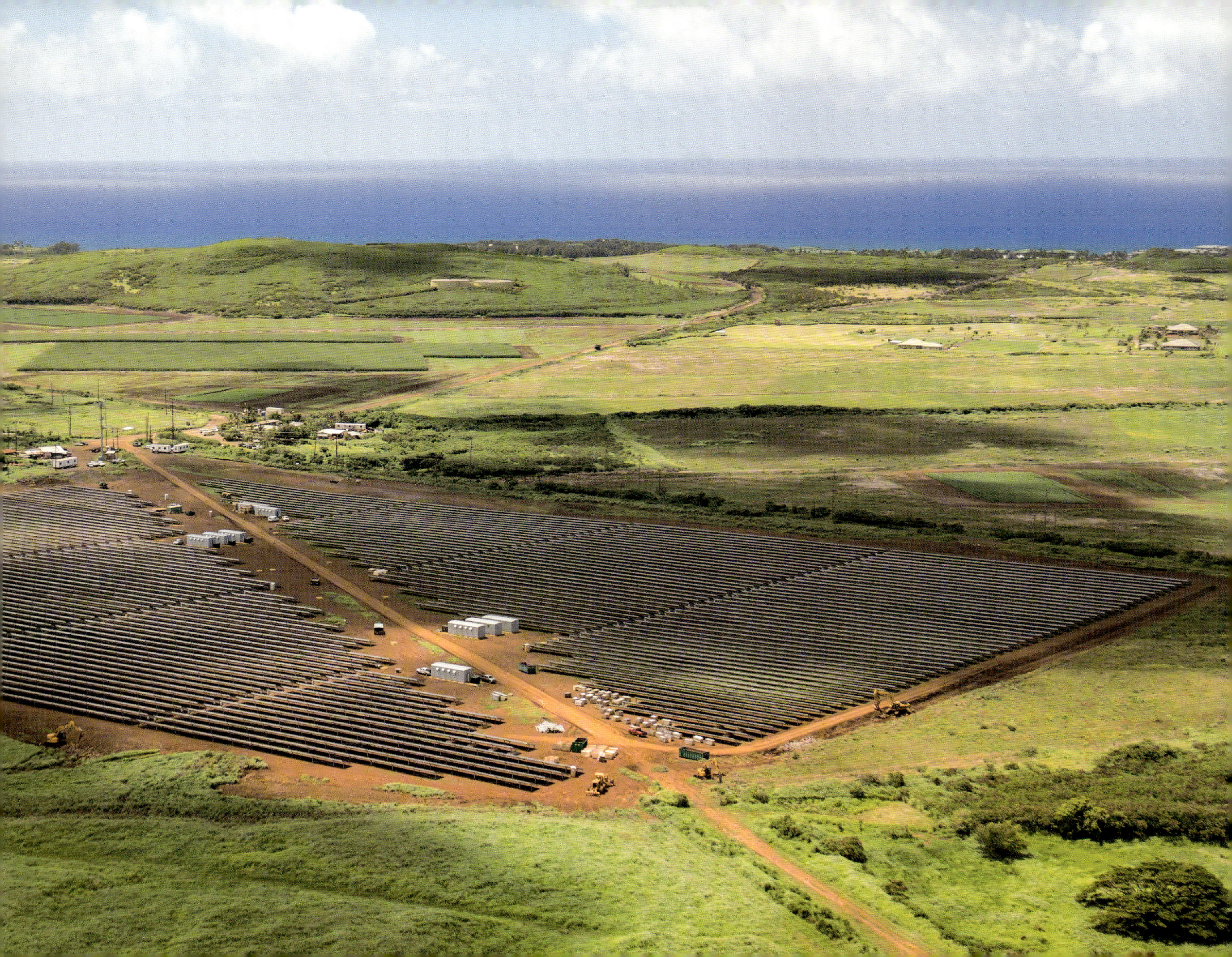

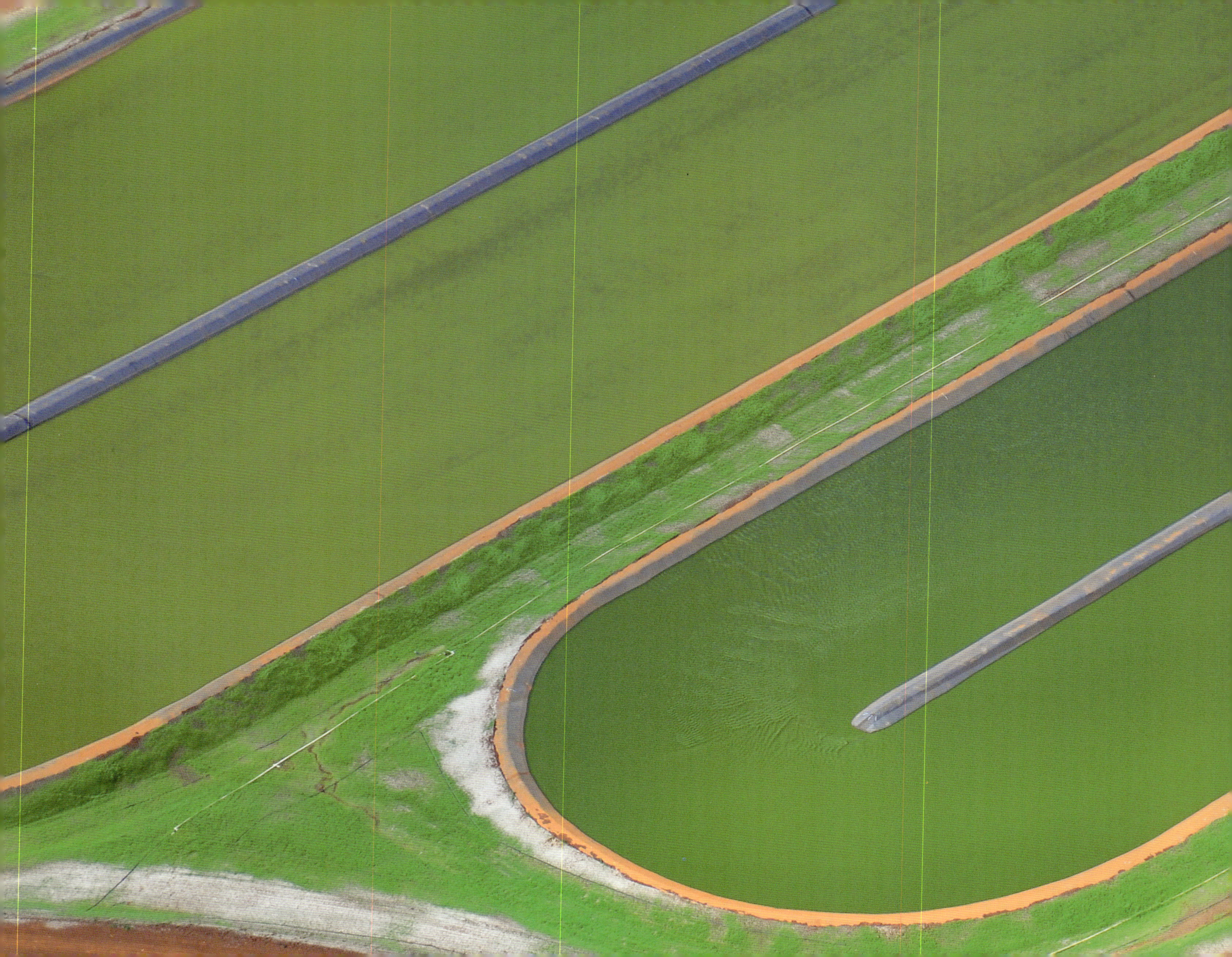

Pacific Gateway Center

Grove Farm is helping human trafficking victims find work through its participation in the Pacific Gateway Center, which serves clients on several islands. (http://www.pacificgatewaycenter.org/)

"We have been longtime supporters for a variety of agricultural initiatives and we were proud to collaborate with Pacific Gateway Center," said Warren Haruki.

"Pacific Gateway Center (PGC) has supported and assisted underserved populations of immigrants, including human trafficking victims. PGC's work through farming, education, training, mentoring and land lease or acquisition activities will enhance the chances of successful self-employment in farming.

"Grove Farm understands that the goals of projects such as PGC's are to empower the production of local agriculture while stimulating entrepreneurial activity. These goals are consistent with the values that Grove Farm is trying to promote on Kaua'i."

Clients of Pacific Gateway Center currently grow a range of truck crops on nine acres of Grove Farm land mauka of Līhu'e.

Līhu'e-Puhi Master Plan Area

Much of the affordable housing, market housing, recreational, industrial, retail and commercial land in the Līhu'e-Puhi master plan area has been developed. It includes the Puakea Golf Course and affiliated facilities.

The company is continuing to work on additional housing projects for local families within the planning area.

The Puakea project includes three phases in the area around the golf course clubhouse and it

---

Left: Hawai'i BioEnergy operates eight acres of algae ponds on thirty-three acres of Grove Farm land adjacent to Kaua'i Island Utility Cooperative's Kapaia power plant. Hawai'i BioEnergy, in which Grove Farm is a partner, works with Texas A&M University and Global Algae Innovations on food supplement and fuel uses for farm-grown algae.

THE INITIATIVES

also includes the site of the former Grove Farm manager's house, which is populated with rows of royal palms as well as numerous fruit trees and other plantings including mango, golden bamboo and chicle. The project is to include sixty-nine house lots.

A second project, Waiola, lies at the eastern end of the Līhu'e-Puhi project, above Nāwiliwili Harbor. Its three phases lie along the lower end of the Puakea Golf Course. They are to include 197 lots.

Wailani

Grove Farm's Wailani project lies along both sides of Ahukini Road, between the Walmart store and Lihue Airport and between Molokoa and the Hanamā'ulu Valley rim. The company's goal with Wailani is to create a sustainable center with residential, retail and other amenities that Līhu'e needs.

The goal is a walkable and bicycle-friendly community that has the feeling of old Līhu'e town, but includes modern planning principles. It should include advanced sustainability technologies and an efficient, compact design.

"Our lands are at the heart of the island. Wailani is ideal for housing, transportation and lifestyle. Our intent is to address the local market. It will be affordable and will bring people back into Līhu'e," Haruki said.

Wailani as a whole has 454 acres and space for 1,360 single and multi-family units. The company divides the project into three parcels:

• Wailani Phase 1, generally the area between Molokoa and Ahukini Road and Kapule Highway. It has seventy-two acres of residential and forty acres of commercial, with more than seven acres of public and park uses.

• Ahukini Mauka, running along the north side

Right: *The treatment plant at the Kapaia Reservoir uses advanced filtration technology to convert surface water to drinkable water for the Līhu'e region. Opened in 2005, the plant treats three million gallons daily and may be expanded by a million or more gallons in the future.*

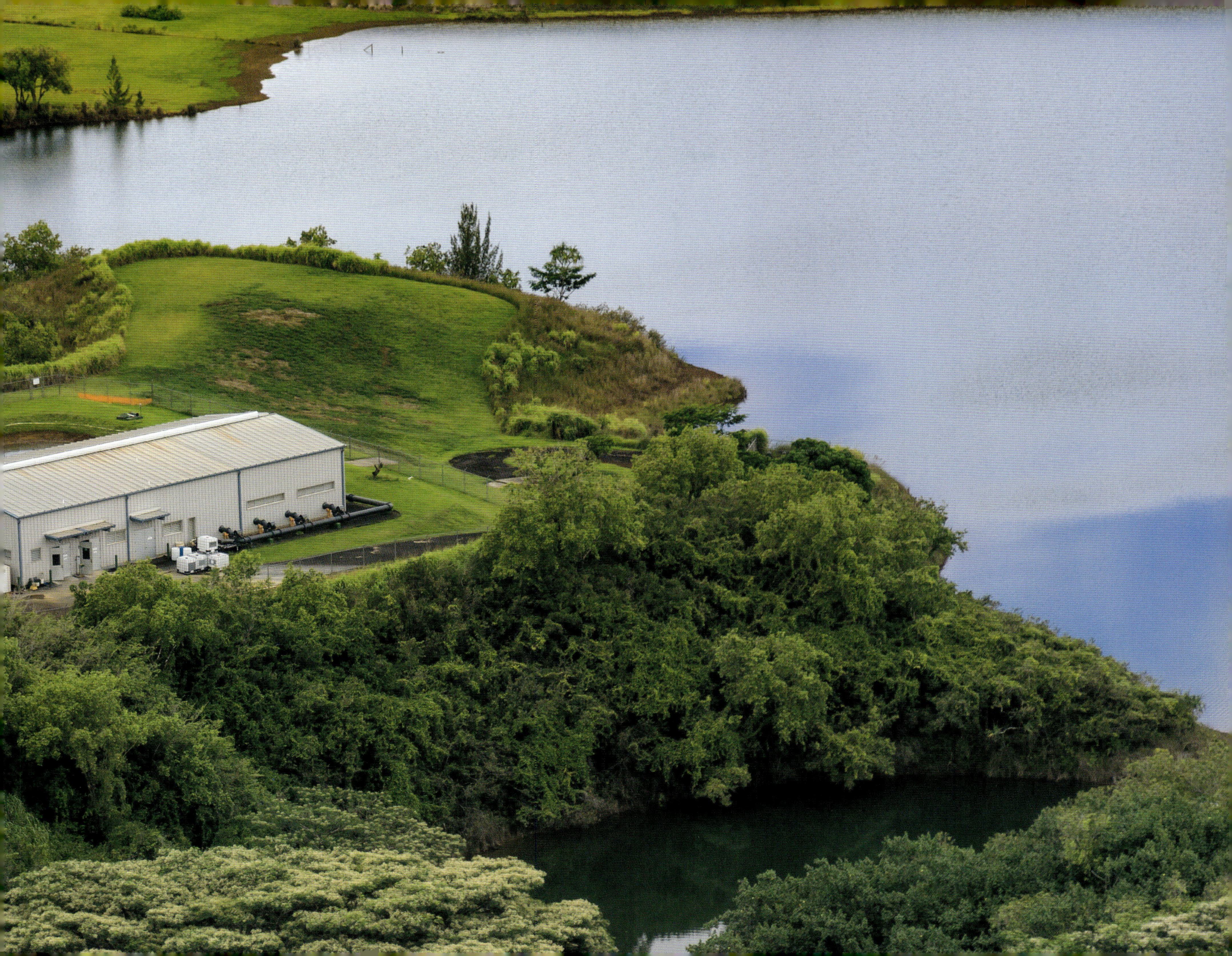

of Ahukini Road between Walmart and Kapule Highway. It includes 133 acres of residential, with thirty-seven acres of commercial, thirteen acres of industrial and twenty-six acres of park and public uses.

• Ahukini Makai, the area between Kapule Highway and Lihue Airport that will be primarily industrial lots. Some of those lots have been committed to the State Department of Transportation to be used in airport-linked functions. Grove Farm is considering an eco-park on part of the property.

"We have studied a lot of energy technologies involved in home construction, and as we get on with the Wailani project, we'll probably employ some of those," Haruki said.

Dan Case added, "It will be an asset, a valuable part of Līhu'e, with affordable housing, a commercial center, banks and other amenities."

Waihohonu

The site of one of the historic Koloa Plantation camps, on the stream that once powered one of Koloa Plantation's sugar mills, is the location for Grove Farm's Waihohonu project.

The former residents of the plantation camp will be offered homes in Waihohonu, where Grove Farm will sell house-and-lot packages at prices designated as affordable for those with incomes of eighty to 140 percent of the median Kaua'i household income.

Grove Farm vice president Dave Hinazumi said the forty-six homes will be of wood frame construction, using factory precut technologies to reduce costs.

"With some of our other subdivisions, we were finding that people were surprised by the cost of construction when they had to build themselves. We can get a better price if we do it as a company," he said.

Grove Farm Foundation

Grove Farm has been funding its 501 (c) (3) charitable foundation with roughly $250,000 annually. Earlier this year, the Foundation had about $3 million.

The money is used for several charitable purposes, including supporting education through scholarships to Kaua'i students.

Each year, Grove Farm donates a college scholarship to three Kaua'i students who are graduating from one of the island's three public high schools and plan to attend four-year college programs. Currently the value of the scholarship is $20,000 per student, distributed at $5,000 per year over four years.

It is a merit-based scholarship, and the selection criteria recognize community service, good citizenship, academic accomplishments and quality of character. It is among the largest scholarship programs in the state of Hawai'i.

To keep the scholarship, students must submit their college transcripts annually and must also perform a minimum amount of community service work each month.

Grove Farm also encourages its employees to participate in community activities and has established its Employee Volunteer Grants program. In this program, employees who perform substantial amounts of volunteer time to certified organizations can obtain two unrestricted $500 grants to those organizations.

The Grove Farm website states: "Moving forward, the Grove Farm Foundation is focused on building communities through leadership;

promoting employee volunteerism; supporting educational enrichment opportunities; enhancing and protecting the environment; assisting health and human service projects; and creating economic opportunities for Kaua'i's future."

Waiahi Water Treatment Plant

Grove Farm is required by the County Department of Water to develop new water sources to meet the needs of its residential, retail and other developments. Such water traditionally would be provided through wells, but during the 1990s, extensive drilling and study found the water levels under the Līhu'e area appeared to be dropping.

Some hydrologists have suggested that Līhu'e's groundwater resources had been artificially increased through a century of furrow irrigation of sugar cane, which delivered tens of millions of gallons of stream water to the fields. Much of that water percolated down to the Līhu'e area aquifer. Once furrow irrigation was replaced by more efficient drip irrigation and when sugar ended production, the aquifer under the Līhu'e region returned to its lower normal levels.

Since wells were not promising sources of consistent water supplies, Grove Farm looked into treating surface water instead. It had rich water resources in the form of the sugar plantation irrigation systems, some of which date to George N. Wilcox's time.

Grove Farm used irrigation water to supply drinking-water supplies with its Waiahi Surface Water Treatment Plant. The facility uses a unique technology, a membrane filtration system developed by General Electric.

In this plant, water from the Kapaia Reservoir is pre-treated to remove most sediment. Then the water is drawn through thousands of membrane filters that remove even microscopic particles. The ZeeWeed Ultrafiltraton Membrane System removes bacteria and other materials with molecular weights of greater than 300,000 through hollow fiber membranes with pore sizes from .04 to .1 microns. The filtered water is chlorinated and delivered to the County Department of Water transmission lines.

The 200- to 300-million-gallon Kapaia reservoir is fed by a ditch system that delivers water from 'Ili'ili'ula, Waikoko and Waiahi Streams as well as smaller streams. The treatment plant was built in 2005 and is capable of consistently producing three million gallons daily of potable water. It is fully automated and can be controlled remotely.

Grove Farm has plans to expand its capacity by another million gallons and perhaps more to meet the requirements of the company's various development proposals.

Ha'ikū

Grove Farm's sale of Ha'ikū land to Cumberland & Western Resources LLC came out of the blue. It was not a parcel that Grove Farm had intended to market, but once the Mainland company made an offer and explained its plans, it seemed to make sense, the Cases and Haruki said.

The buyer, which owns hundreds of thousands of acres across the country, has agreed to keep the land in agriculture, which was a condition of the deal.

"We had no plans to sell these 2,700 acres, but when we were approached by Cumberland & Western Resources and learned of their intended use—which includes agricultural research and production—and when they agreed to make that commitment a condition of the sale, we decided to move forward," Haruki said.

The Ha'ikū lands lie in an arc on the northern side of the western end of the Hā'upu Range. They are part of the second big purchase of property that George Norton Wilcox made as he built his plantation.

Dan Case said, "It was not a planned thing. It was not land you could do much with. It's hard to get anything rezoned. If you lease it out, all you get is somebody paying your real property taxes and maintenance. So when an interested party came along, saying they wanted to buy the land to keep it in agriculture, Warren (Haruki) showed him what we had. They agreed to keep it in agriculture and we have the first right to buy it back. They paid about $16 million and we used it to pay off a lot of debt."

For Steve Case, the deciding factor was that Cumberland & Western Resources did not want to develop the land, but had some innovative ideas for using it sustainably. Details of its plans had not been revealed publicly at this writing.

Haruki said, "This sale builds on the commitment Grove Farm has made to the Kaua'i community over the past 150 years, including our recent decision to voluntarily designate half of all of our lands to permanent agricultural use. We believe Cumberland & Western Resources will be a responsible steward of these lands and an important contributor to the Kaua'i community."

Cumberland & Western Resources president Bill Murphree said the goal is not simply to land bank the property: "With our future plans for this site, it is our hope that we will be able to positively contribute to the island's economic diversity and promote efforts towards global sustainability."

Important Agricultural Land

Grove Farm, after the sale to Cumberland & Western Resources, has about 38,000 acres of land on Kaua'i. It makes Steve Case the largest individual landowner on Kaua'i and second only statewide to Larry Ellison, who owns most of the island of Lāna'i.

Grove Farm has dedicated a third of Case's Kaua'i

> *The buyer did not want to develop the land but had innovative ideas for using it sustainably.*

holdings to permanent agricultural use under the State's Important Agricultural Land program. The company in 2011 dedicated 1,533 acres around Māhā'ulepū. Then in 2013, it dedicated another 11,048 acres held by two Case companies: Grove Farm and Hā'upu Land.

At the same time, Grove Farm gave up an important development concession on those properties. The Important Agricultural Land program allows landowners to reclassify to urban or rural up to fifteen percent of the acreage dedicated. Grove Farm waived that right.

For Steve Case, that is simply part of the tradition of the 150-year-old company.

"Try to build on the past with an eye on the future. Try to be respectful of the legacy of the past and recognize that some of the lessons from that can help form the future. It is a long-term commitment, has been and will continue to be," Case said.

"My dad's legacy and to some extent our family legacy lives on. We're trying to be good stewards and good citizens of the community, trying to do some things that move things forward." 🌿

Right: *Grove Farm's verdant lands on the eastern slopes of Kilohana Crater are a blend of valleys and plains, forests and pastures, all flowing down to the island's urban center at Līhu'e.*

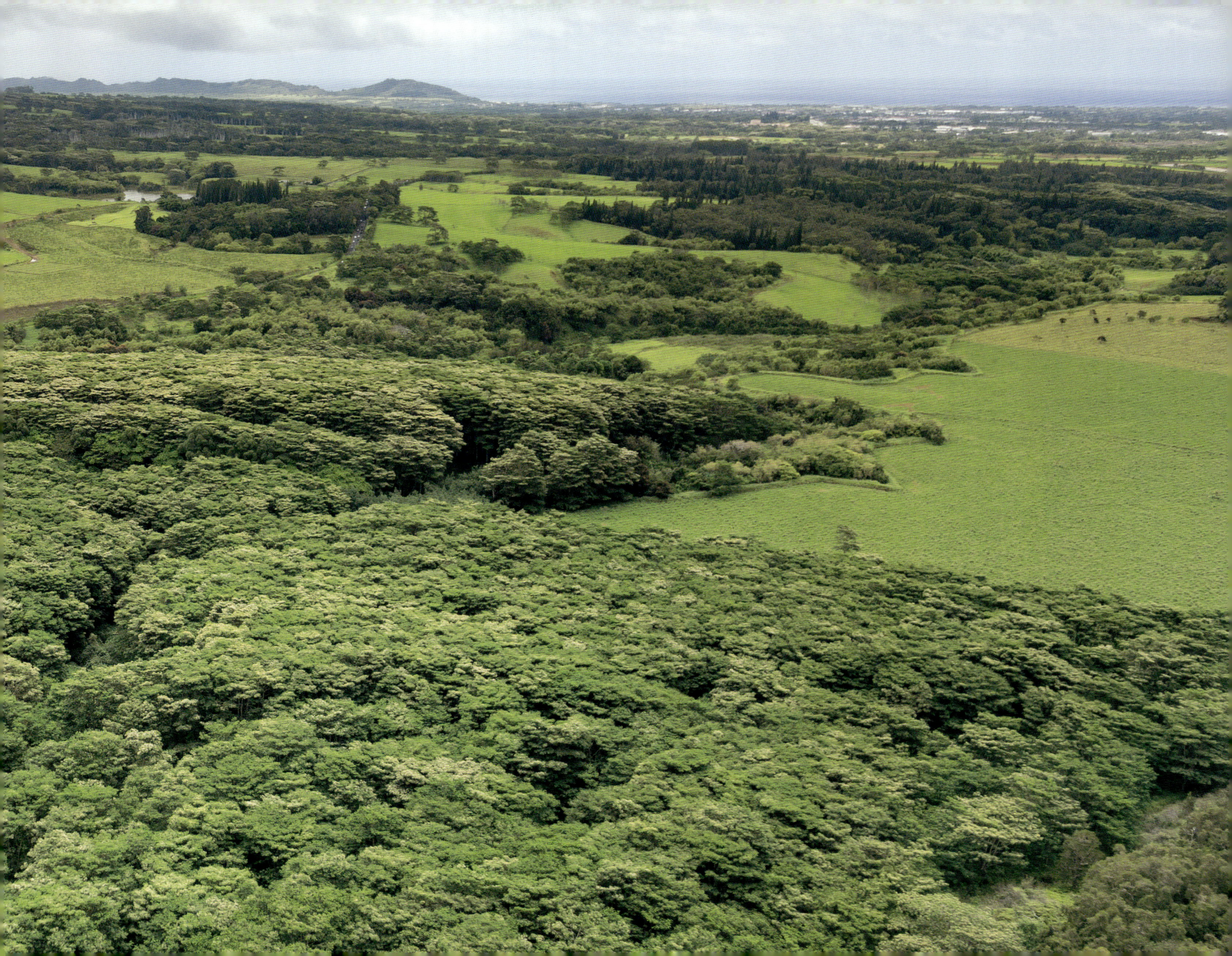

Epilogue

"Celebrate the past, live in the present and lean into the future." —Steve Case

One of the themes of this book is the many ways in which the Grove Farm of 150 years ago is the logical ancestor of today's company.

The differences, of course, are manifest.

Thatched roofs, schooners and oxcarts were everyday life back then. Ledgers were handwritten in the light of a flickering flame. George Norton Wilcox, as forward thinking a man as he was, would have been speechless at today's world.

But the similarities between Wilcox's pre-industrial sugar farm and today's modern company are intriguing. In a speech before the Chamber of Commerce of Hawai'i in 2014, Steve Case underscored that message.

"Celebrate the past, live in the present and lean into the future," he said.

George Norton Wilcox probably wouldn't have used exactly those words, but the message would have resonated with him. He regularly looked into his own history for answers to problems that were troubling him in the present. For example, as a young man he had dug guano, and when he later faced soil fertility issues on his Kaua'i sugar plantation, he looked to the natural fertilizer on the bird rookeries of the northwestern Hawaiian Islands.

Wilcox was a man who lived in the here and now. He enjoyed a drink and a cigar. ("Good for the digestion," he said.) He was a fast friend to innumerable island residents of every race and class. He was famous for stopping for a friendly chat along the roadside as he went about Grove Farm business.

And hardly anyone of his time leaned into the future as much as George Norton Wilcox, the great planner who adopted and even invented new technology, backed steamship lines, built harbors, funded schools and donated to numerous churches of religions not his own.

Today's Grove Farm lives its history. It has restored the old plantation estate at Iliahi, built a sanctuary for endangered bird species and engaged the community in ecological restoration with the planting of thousands of native trees, plants and shrubs. It is finding new uses for the infrastructure built during Wilcox's time. It has dedicated much of its land to farming in perpetuity.

The company is engaged in cutting-edge technologies for food and agricultural production. It is developing subdivisions and building housing for today's families. Its employees are encouraged to participate in community organizations and activities.

Grove Farm is actively involved in finding ways to guide us to a more sustainable future, whether by participating in the state's largest solar farm or partnering with others to make fuel out of pond scum.

And through its foundation today's Grove Farm is contributing to education as G.N. Wilcox did. Its Wailani project uses forward-thinking planning principles to create a green community that will be walkable and bicycle-friendly. It is working with landowning, investment and energy partners to help the island of Kaua'i move into a sustainable energy future.

They are separated in time by a century and a half. The tools and the individual projects might be very different. But Steve Case's Grove Farm is a company George Wilcox would easily have recognized as the heir to his vision back in 1864.

—Jan W. TenBruggencate

Grove Farm—Koloa Sugar rail completion, Knudsen Gap, 1930

Grove Farm Archive

Ox team with cart, 1919

Grove Farm manager Fred Smith and son Raymond with cane cars, 1895

Bullock carts, Makaweli, 1890

Nāwiliwili Harbor, 1928

Hule'ia River railroad bridge under construction, 1909

Workers on Hule'ia River railroad bridge, 1909

Steam plow, Makaweli, 1905

Knapsack weed spray crew, 1939

GROVE FARM ARCHIVE

E.H.W. Broadbent (right) with high-clearance cultivator, 1924

Spinner-type weed cultivator, 1928

Tractor cultivator used from 1920 to 1930

Flume installation, 1933

Puhi hollow tile plant, ca. 1937

Sprayer sled, 1939

Rider Joe Gomes with chain-type cane car, 1944

Flame cultivator for weed control, 1946

Līhu'e, 1915

Gov. Wallace Farrington, Nāwiliwili Harbor dedication, 1921

First irrigated land planter in Territory of Hawai'i, 1923

Grove Farm office, Puhi, 1934

Koloa Sugar Company centennial celebration, 1935

County Council chair Anthony Baptiste accepts Pua Loke playground deed from Albert Wilcox, 1952

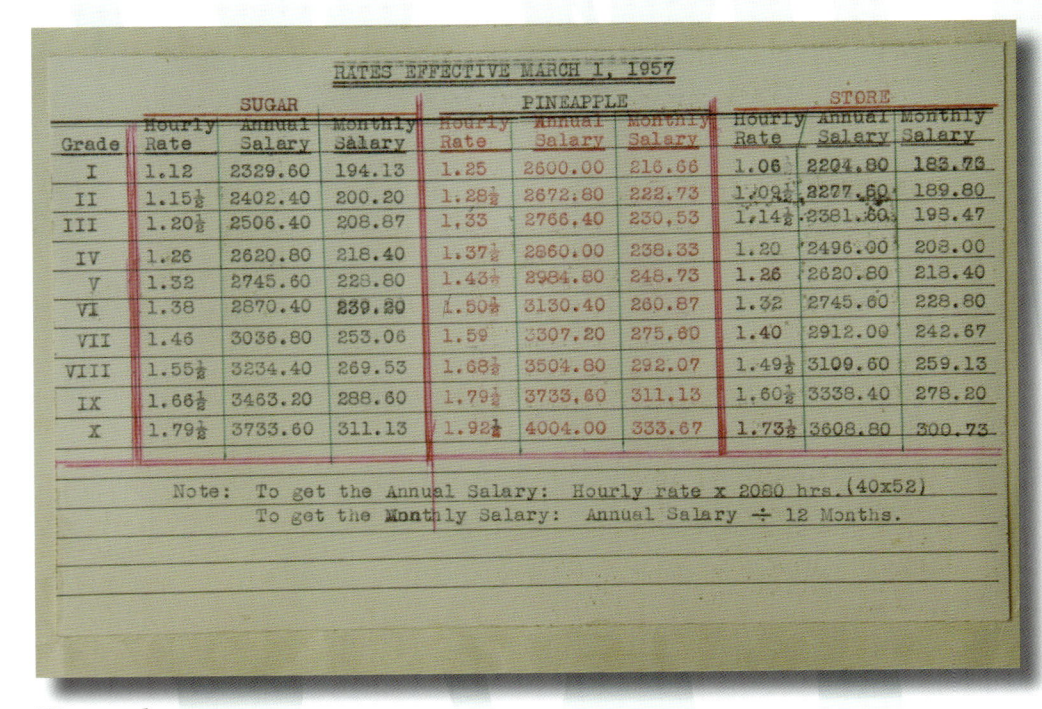

Wage scale, 1957

Plantation house scale model, Kaua'i County Fair, 1938

GROVE FARM ARCHIVE 131

Hawai'i's first cane seed planter, 1922

Cane seed replanter, 1945

Cane seed replanter, 1945

Pineapple harvester, 1945

Pineapple harvester, 1945

Pineapple harvester conveyor boom, 1945

Pineapple havesting, 1945

Moragne Seed Cutter, 1947

Moragne Seed Cutter with five saws, 1947

Moragne Seed Cutter crew, 1947

Chemical weed control crew, 1947

Koloa planter, 1948

W.M. Moragne, Wilcox Tunnel, 1948

Blue rock quarry and crushing plant, 1949

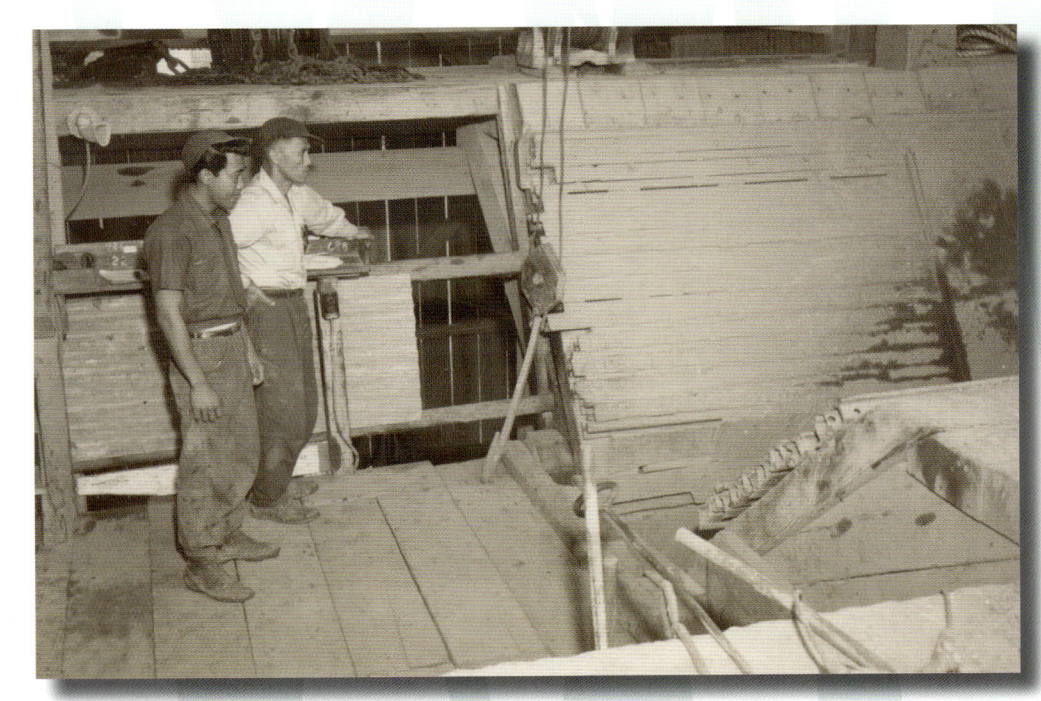

Blue rock quarry and crushing plant, 1949

Koloa Mill boiling house, 1950

Long-hose herbicide spray unit, 1948

Cane haul road construction, 1948

Wilcox Tunnel drill set-up, 1948

Wilcox Tunnel excavation, 1949

Wilcox Tunnel hydraulic drilling, 1949

Seedling distribution, 1949

Blue rock quarry and crushing plant, 1949

Blue rock quarry, 1949

Koloa field irrigation pump, 1950

Waikomo Bridge, 1952

George Jottmann, Koloa Mill, 1952

Last locomotive leaves Koloa Mill, 1952

Koloa Mill cane cleaning plant, 1953

Koloa Mill cane cleaning plant, 1955

Koloa Mill cane cleaning plant remodeling, 1955

Erection of Koloa Mill smokestack, 1954

GROVE FARM ARCHIVE 139

Tractor cultivator used from 1920 to 1930

A.H. Case, S.W. Wilcox, W.M. Moragne, W.P. Alexander, 1943

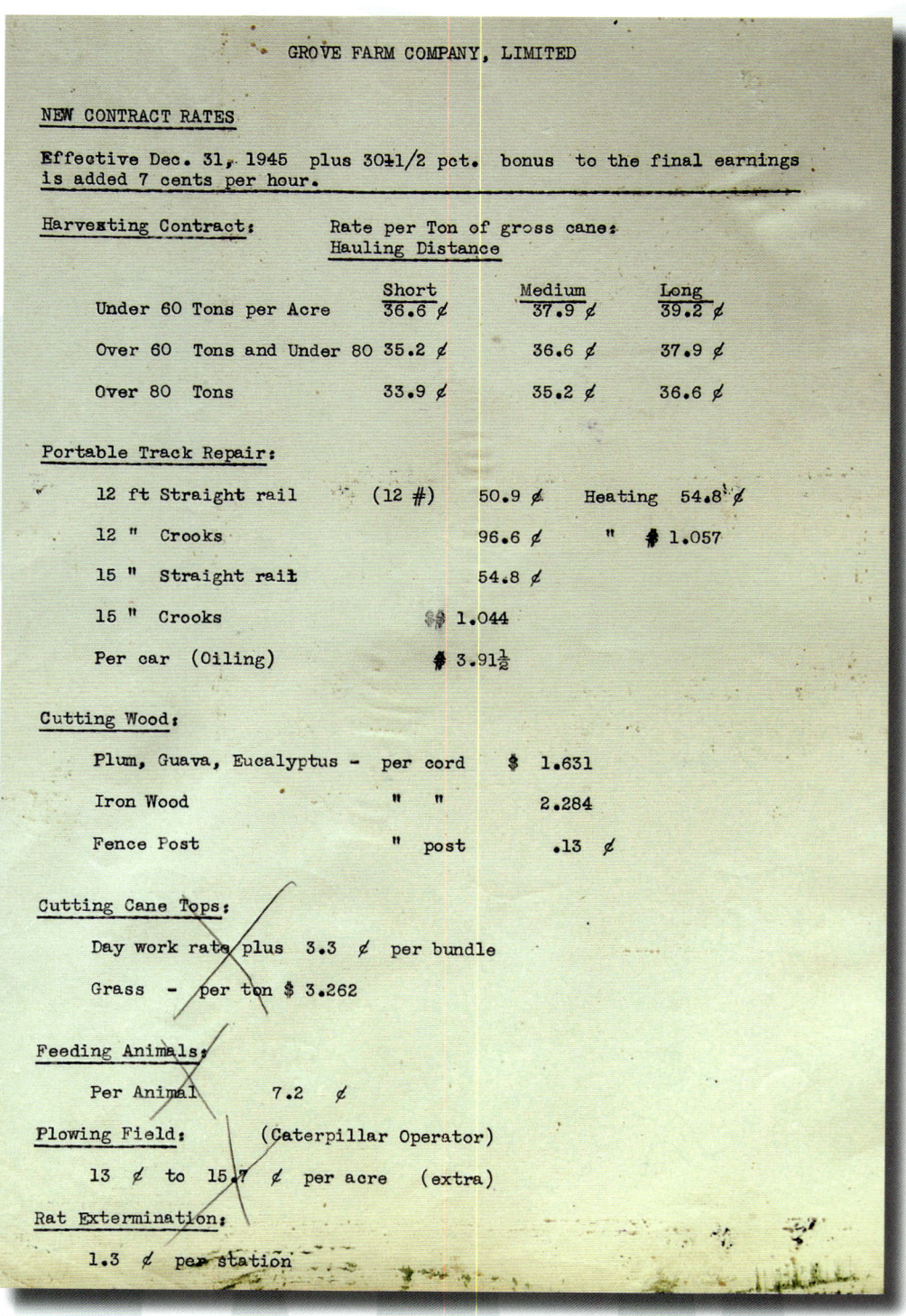

GROVE FARM COMPANY, LIMITED

NEW CONTRACT RATES

Effective Dec. 31, 1945 plus 30-1/2 pct. bonus to the final earnings is added 7 cents per hour.

Harvesting Contract: Rate per Ton of gross cane:

Hauling Distance

	Short	Medium	Long
Under 60 Tons per Acre	36.6 ¢	37.9 ¢	39.2 ¢
Over 60 Tons and Under 80	35.2 ¢	36.6 ¢	37.9 ¢
Over 80 Tons	33.9 ¢	35.2 ¢	36.6 ¢

Portable Track Repair:

12 ft Straight rail   (12 #)   50.9 ¢   Heating 54.8 ¢

12 " Crooks   96.6 ¢   " $1.057

15 " Straight rail   54.8 ¢

15 " Crooks $1.044

Per car (Oiling) $3.91½

Cutting Wood:

Plum, Guava, Eucalyptus - per cord $1.631

Iron Wood   "   "   2.284

Fence Post   " post   .13 ¢

Cutting Cane Tops:

Day work rate plus 3.3 ¢ per bundle

Grass - per ton $3.262

Feeding Animals:

Per Animal   7.2 ¢

Plowing Field: (Caterpillar Operator)

13 ¢ to 15.7 ¢ per acre (extra)

Rat Extermination:

1.3 ¢ per station

Grove Farm contract rates, 1945

Dedication Ceremonies
Nāwiliwili Breakwater
OCTOBER 28, 1921 3 P.M.

Program

INTRODUCTORY	H. D. Wishard
	President Kauai Chamber of Commerce
LAYING FIRST CAP STONE	G. N. Wilcox
ADDRESS	Hon. W. R. Farrington
	Governor of Hawaii

The above exercises to be interspersed with Fireworks by the Japanese Community

---

Banquet Session Kauai Chamber of Commerce

in

Celebration of Commencement of Construction

of

Nāwiliwili Breakwater

Lihue Armory 6:30 P.M.

Program

WELCOME	Rev. R. W. Bayless
ADDRESS	Maj. Gen. Charles P. Summerall
RESPONSE	Sam Carter
	Post Commander, American Legion
ADDRESS	Hon. J. K. Kalanianaole
CONGRATULATORY REMARKS	S. Yamada
ADDRESS	Hon. W. R. Farrington

MUSIC BY ORCHESTRA

Nāwiliwili Breakwater dedication program, 1921

Limestone crushing plant, 1952

Blue rock quarry plant, 1949

Bibliography

Alexander, Arthur C., *Koloa Plantation: 1835-1935*, 2nd ed. Līhu'e, Kauai Historical Society, 1985 (original 1937).

Cathcart, James, *Bauxite Deposits of Hawaii, Maui and Kauai, Territory of Hawaii, A Preliminary Report*, U.S. Geological Survey, 1958.

Damon, Ethel, *Interviews with George N. Wilcox*, oral history housed at Grove Farm Homestead Museum.

Donohugh, Donald, *The Story of Kōloa: A Kaua'i Plantation Town*, Mutual Publishing, Honolulu, 2001.

Dorrance, WIlliam H., *Sugar Islands*, Mutual Publishing, Honolulu, 2001.

Grove Farm annual reports, various years.

Grove Farm Homestead Museum archives, including oral histories of William P. Alexander, A. Hebard Case, Gaylord P. Wilcox, George N. Wilcox.

Grove Farm Plantation News, various editions, housed at Grove Farm Homestead Museum.

Hawai'i Agricultural Experiment Station annual reports, various years.

Hawai'i Intermediate Court of Appeals No. 28626 (Civil No. 02-1-0182) Ralph Hart Fisher, et al, v. Grove Farm Company et al.

Hawai'i Intermediate Court of Appeals No. 28772 (Civil No. 02-1-0182) Keith Tsukamoto, et al, v. Grove Farm Company, et al.

Hawai'i Intermediate Court of Appeals Nos. 25811, 26030, Michael G. Sheehan, Sr., v. Grove Farm Company, et al.

The Honolulu Advertiser, Amfac files bankruptcy in twilight of 'Big Five', Thursday, February 28, 2002.

Joesting, Edward, *Kauai: The Separate Kingdom*, University of Hawai'i Press, Honolulu, 1984.

Krauss, Bob, with W.P. Alexander, *Grove Farm Plantation: The Biography of a Hawaiian Sugar Plantation*, 2nd ed., Pacific Books, Palo Alto, California, 1984 (original Grove Farm Company 1965).

Larsen, Jack L., with Dr. Thomas A. Marks, *Hawaiian Pineapple Entrepreneurs 1894-2010*, Jack L. Larsen, 2010.

The Pacific Commercial Advertiser, November 5, 1864.

The Polynesian, September 19, 1857.

Pukui, Mary Kawena, Samuel H. Elbert, Esther T. Mookini, *Place Names of Hawaii*, University Press of Hawai'i, Honolulu.

TenBruggencate, Jan, *The Legacy of EHW Broadbent, A History*, A Pratt Published Book, Līhu'e, 2009.

TenBruggencate, Jan, *Lihue Mill: Grinding Cane and Building Community*, Pahio Develoment & Lihue MS LLC, Līhu'e, 2011.

Wilcox, Carol, *Sugar Water: Hawaii's Plantation Ditches*, University of Hawai'i Press, Honolulu, 1997.

Index

Abines, Laureano, 8
Agee, John, 94, 100
Agena, Robert H. "Bobby," 66-67, 69-70
Agena, Shiro, 67
Agustin, Demetrio "Deme," 38, 68
Agustin, Potenciano "Pat," 3, 38, 66, 68-70
Agustin, Timoteo, 38
Ahukini Terminal and Railway Company, 62
Ahung, 36
Alaska Permanent Fund, 97
Albero, Magno, 44
Alexander & Baldwin, 32, 74-75
Alexander, Arthur C., 36
Alexander, Samuel, 15
Alexander, William P., 20, 26, 30, 53, 107, 140
ALPS Investment LLC, 94
Amby Fernandez Store, 38
American Factors (Amfac), 14, 26, 30, 51, 62, 74-75, 103
American Sugar Refining Company, 15
Amfac Sugar Company, 75
AOL, 89, 94-96
AOL Time Warner, 3
Armstrong, W.N., 107
Aspen Venture Group, 88
Atai, 36
Atlantic Dairy Consulting, LLC, 109

Baldwin, Henry P., 15
Bank of Hawai'i, 83, 85, 97
Baptiste, Anthony, 131
Bargo, Vincente, 70
Belt Collins & Associates, 81-82
Berg, Karl, 75
Bishop Bank, 54
Bishop Estate, 13
Bishop, Bernice Pauahi, 13, 54
Bishop, Charles Reed, 54
Blum, Scott A., 85, 88-89
Brandt, Herman, 70
Brinsmade, Peter Allan, 36
Britton, Leonard, 29
Broadbent, E.H.W. "Ned", 3, 12, 19-20, 26-27, 32, 82, 96, 128, 147
Burbank, Samuel, 6, 37-39
Burnham, Charles, 37
Burns, Caleb E.S., 47, 56, 61
Butler, Gladys, 81

Buy.com, 88

C. Brewer & Co., 54, 74, 90
Cacabelos, Avelardo "Manok" "Chick", 3, 66-68, 70
California and Hawaiian (C&H) Sugar Company, 15, 21
Carswell, Donn A., 3, 88, 94
Case Bigelow & Lombardi, 89, 94
Case, Aderial Hebard "Hib", 3, 6, 19-20, 26, 30, 90, 95
Case, Bill, 20, 90
Case, Daniel, 3, 6, 19-20, 75, 80-83, 85, 87, 89-90, 94-97, 99-100, 102, 108-109, 118-119
Case, Jim, 20, 90
Case, Marie, 95
Case, Steve, 1-3, 5-7, 19-21, 35, 62, 80, 82, 86-87, 89-90, 94-97, 99-100, 102, 108-109, 118-119, 120, 122-123
Case/McConnell, Elizabeth, 20
Central Pacific Bank, 97
Chaney Brooks, 85
Charman, George, 38
Chinen, Remedios "Remy" Alayvilla, 3, 81
Colburn, John F., 16
Costco, 102, 104
Cox, Howard, 68
Cropp, Anton, 38-39, 44
Cropp, Ernest, 44, 47
Cumberland & Western Resources LLC, 16, 119

Dairy Solutionz (NZ) Ltd., 109
Damon, Ethel, 15
Daub, Rhye, 3
Defense Advanced Research Projects Agency, 109
Department of Water, 119
Dods, Walter, 97
Dohrman, Pamela W., 88
Dole, George, 38
Dole, Sanford, 19
Domino Foods, 15
Dowsett, Jack, 6
Ellison, Larry, 120
Eric Knudsen Estate, 31, 75
Farrington, Wallace, 130
Fern, Charles J., 10, 16, 20
Fern, Mike, 20

Finistere Ventures, 109
First Hawaiian Bank, 54, 83, 85, 97
Francisco de Paula Marin, Don, 36
Fukumoto, Kakuichi, 44
Funada Store, 38
Funaku, Michiye Fujimoto, 3, 29, 65, 67, 70, 95
Funaku, Stanley, 95
Furukawa, Charles, 70
Furukawa, Chester, 68

Galante, Nick, 3
Gay & Robinson, 74
Gayagas, Boyd, 3
Gayagas, Gaylene, 3
General Atomics, 109
General Electric, 119
Giacometti, Guido, 82-83, 85
Gillin, Elbert T., 26
Global Algae Innovations, 109, 115
Gomes, Joe, 129
Goodale, Warren, 7
Grove Farm Foundation, 1, 97, 102, 118-119
Grove Farm Homestead Museum, 3-4, 7, 9-10, 13, 14, 25, 32, 37, 39, 42, 49, 70, 81, 89, 103
Gulick, Charles T., 16

Haneberg, Adolf, 38
Haruki, Warren, 1, 3, 96-97, 109, 112, 115-116, 118-119
Hashimoto, Harry, 68
Hawai'i Agricultural Experiment Station, 21
Hawai'i BioEnergy, LLC, 109, 112, 115
Hawaii Dairy Farms, 107-109
Hawaiian Airlines, 15
Hawaiian Electric Company, 109
Hawaiian Fruit Packers/Hawaiian Canneries, 27, 95
Hawaiian Sugar Planters Association, 95
HC&D, 51
Hinazumi, David, 3, 118
Holyroyde, Eddie, 75
Honolulu Iron Works, 34, 44
Honu Group, 88-89, 94
Hooper, William, 36-37
Hungtai, 36

Iliahi Estate, 56, 103, 107, 123

Interisland Airways, 15
Inter-Island Steam Navigation Company, 15, 19
Isenberg, Hans, 39
Isenberg, Paul R., 10, 12, 14-15, 38-39, 52-54, 61
Island Strategy LLC, 147

Jas. W. Glover Ltd., 85
JMB Realty, 62
Jottmann, George, 138
Judd, Charlie, 107
Judd, Frank, 107
Kaikioewa, 36
Kalākaua, David, 16, 107
Kamāmalu, Victoria, 54
Kamehameha I, 13
Kamehameha III (Kauikeaouli), 6, 36
Kamehameha Schools, 13, 109
Kaneshiro, Arryl, 3
Kapoli, Kaumana "Mary", 6
Kaua'i Invasive Species Committee, 103
Kaua'i Island Utility Cooperative, 109, 112-113, 115, 147
Kauai Pineapple Company, 27, 111
Ke'elikōlani, Ruth, 13
Kealia Plantation, 39
Kekaha Sugar Company, 14, 54, 74, 111
Kentron, 111
Khosla Ventures, 109
Khosla, Vinod, 109
Kilauea Sugar, 74
Kilpatrick-Rigg, Leah, 100
Kipu Plantation, 59, 62
Klebahn, Hugh, 82, 85, 88-89, 94
Kmart, 104
Knudsen, Valdemar, 75
Koloa Plantation, 3, 7, 9, 25, 30-32, 24-51, 54, 62, 66, 70, 97, 118
Koloa Store, 39, 71
Koloa Sugar Company, 1, 3, 34, 49, 51, 59, 66, 131
Kuboyama, Koji, 69
Kurasaki, Kazu, 68

Labrador, Andres, 51
Labrador, Perfecto, 3, 51, 66-67, 69-70
Ladd & Co., 36-37, 54
Ladd, William, 36

Lam Yuen, Sharyl, 3
Larsen, Jack, 27
Lawrence, Fred, 95
Lee, William L., 54
Lehman Brothers, 89
Liberty House, 80
Lihue Land Co., 62, 102
Lihue Plantation, 1, 3, 6-10, 12-14, 25, 30, 38, 44, 47, 52-63, 70, 74-75, 80-81, 97, 147
Liliʻuokalani, Lydia, 16
Lindsey, James N., 37
Longs Drugs, 80

Madayag, Moises, 3
Mahelona, Ethel Kulamanu, 14
Makee Plantation, 25, 62
Makee Sugar Company, 61
Malapit, Eduardo, 68
Marshall, James F.B., 6-7
Marshall, James H. B., 54
Marshall, Tom, 70
Matsunaga, Joel, 109
Maui Land & Pineapple Company, 94, 109
McBryde Sugar Company, 1, 9, 30, 32, 42, 51, 59, 74-75, 80-81
McLane, Patrick, 36, 39, 44
Moir, Alexandra Knudsen, 59
Moir, Gertrude, 59
Moir, Hector, 47, 59
Moir, John T., 47, 59
Moir, John T. "Jack", 59
Moir, John T. III, 9
Moir, Mildred Mae, 59
Moke, Danny, 49
Moore, Randolph G., 88
Moragne, J.H., 62
Moragne, William M., 8, 19-20, 26-27, 29-31, 51, 59, 74, 83, 135, 140
Mullins, Robert D., 88
Muraoka, Taka, 68
Muronaka, Naoki, 70
Murphree, Bill, 119

Napoleon, Sam   31
National Tropical Botanical Garden, 103, 112
Nelson, Lloyd, 59
Nēnē Goose Habitat Initiative, 98, 103, 106-107
Nishihara, Mitsugi, 70

Nishimoto, Egan, 80
Nobriga, David, 3, 29, 59, 67
North Pacifc Phosphate and Fertilizer Company, 13

ʻOhana Holdings, LLC, 109
Okubo, Suemi, 68
Olokele Sugar Company, 74, 95
Omidyar, Pam, 108
Omidyar, Pierre, 108-109
Oshima, Henry, 9, 68
Oshima, Stanley, 68
Otani, Toshihiro, 49
Oyasato, Chisei, 44

Pacific Gateway Center, 102, 115
Pacific Missile Range Facility, 111
Panui, Marion, 67
Patterson, Wilcox, 88
Peirce, Henry A., 54
Peterson, C., 26
Pioneer Mill, 44, 59
Pratt, David W., 3, 19, 30, 73, 75, 80-83, 89, 94-97, 102
Pratt, Dudley Sr., 3, 19-20, 82, 90, 96
Pratt, William D., 88
Pratt, Bill, 96
Pratt, Sam, 96
Prevost, Victor, 37
Property Development Centers, 102
Puhi Store, 68, 95

Racelo, Saturnino, 70
Rapozo, Pat, 15
Rice, Charles, 59
Rice, William Harrison, 6-7, 61
Ripley, Clinton B., 10
Riznik, Barnes, 32
Ruiz, Alexander, 70

Sagun, Alex, 44
Sakoda, Bernadette Hanako Tokuda "Bernie", 3, 65-66, 68-70
Sandblom, Marissa, 3, 107
Sanekane, Yuhie, 70
Sasaki, Masaru, 31
Sasaki, Noboru, 27
Schleck, Bob, 3, 7, 32

Schuler Homes, 82
Science Applications International Corporation, 109
Sears, 80
Semana, Rosita, 39
Shimabukuro, Shawn, 3
Silva, John, 59
Sloggett, Henry Digby, 90
Smith, Allan, 3, 9, 81, 83, 85
Smith, Fred, 126
Smith, Raymond, 126
Smith, W.O., 107
Solar City, 112
Spencer, Charles, 16
Spreckels, Klaus, 15
Star Market, 80
State Department of Land and Natural Resources, 103
State Department of Transportation, 118
State Division of Forestry and Wildlife, 107
Stevens, John L., 19
Sun Len Chong Store, 38
Tabata, Stanley, 80
Texas A&M University, 109, 115
The Home Depot, 102, 104
Thomas, Telesforo, 31
Ti Root Okolehau Hawaii Inc., 30
Time Warner, 89
Tobey Plantation, 36
Tokuda, Mitsue "Nancy", 68
Tokuda, Robert Seiyei, 68
Tze-Chun, Wong, 36

Ulupono Initiative, 108

Van Dreser, Lyle, 20, 67
Vasconcelles, Caesar, 70
Vea, Carlina Tumbaga, 3, 14
Viluan, Stanley, 3, 111

Waiahi Water Treatment Plant, 119
Walmart, 110, 116, 118
Weinberg, Harry, 80, 94
Weinzheimer, Ludwig, 44
Widemann, Hermann A., 6-7, 10, 12, 54
Widemann, Minna, 6
Wilcox, Abner, 26
Wilcox, Albert, 12, 15, 25, 61, 131

Wilcox, Charles H., 25, 39, 44
Wilcox, Elsie, 26
Wilcox, Emma, 12
Wilcox, Etta, 26
Wilcox, Gaylord Parke, 14, 23, 25-26, 29, 30, 35, 39, 53, 73-74, 94-95, 108
Wilcox, George Norton, 1, 3-10, 12-16, 19-20, 25-26, 30, 32, 38-39, 44, 52-54, 61, 70, 73-74, 89-90, 94, 96-97, 100, 102-103, 107, 119, 123
Wilcox, Lucy, 26
Wilcox, Mabel, 20, 26, 32, 90
Wilcox, S.W., 140
Wilcox, Sam, 3-4, 12, 14, 25-26, 32, 74-75, 82, 96, 103
Wilcox, Debbie, 3, 96
Wilder Steamship Company, 15
Wilder, Kimo, 10
Wood, Robert W., 6, 37-38
Wright, John N., 38

Yamada, Satsuyo, 39

MAP OF GROVE FARM
PUNA KAUAI

Owned By Hon. C. N. Wilcox
Scale 500 Feet = 1 Inch
Survey and Map by W. A. Wall
1897